I0814220

DEVOTION *to* OUR LORD *in the* WOMB

DEVOTION *to* OUR LORD *in the* WOMB

The Divine Nine Months

FR. HENRY JAMES COLERIDGE, SJ

TAN Books
Gastonia, North Carolina

Cover design by Jordan Avery

Cover image: *The Visitation* by Raffaello Sanzio of Urbino / Bridgeman Images.

ISBN: 978-1-5051-3604-3
Kindle ISBN: 978-1-5051-3756-9
ePUB ISBN: 978-1-5051-3755-2

Published in the United States by
TAN Books
PO Box 269
Gastonia, NC 28053

www.TANBooks.com

Printed in the United States of America

Virginum custos et pater
Sancte Joseph
Cujus fideli custodiæ
Ipsa innocentia Christus Jesus
Et ipsa Virgo Virginum Maria
Commissa fuit
Te per hoc utrumque carissimum pignus
Jesum et Mariam
Obsecro et obtestor
Ut me ad omni immunditia præservatum
Mente incontaminata
Puro corde et casto corpore
Jesu et Mariæ
Semper facias
Castissime famulari

Contents

Editor's Note

This edition by TAN Books is an abridged version of the original work by Fr. Henry James Coleridge, SJ. While every effort has been made to preserve the spirit and core teachings of the author, certain sections have been condensed or omitted for clarity, accessibility, and length. First published in 1885 by Burns and Oates, the British edition numbered 362 pages without the front matter and appendix. Because the author covered much more ground than the central thesis or subject of his manuscript, the editors decided to greatly shorten the volume so that readers would benefit from the most important and central reflections and meditations of the author on the life of Jesus during Our Lady's nine months of pregnancy. It was also believed that a high-quality abbreviated version would appeal to more readers than the full-length original edition.

The process of shortening this edition involved the substantial reduction in length of existing chapters and the elimination of chapter 12. The chapters have been renumbered. The original British spelling was Americanized. The editorial process included the elimination of some footnotes and thus required the reformatting of the text with renumbered notes. Errors that existed in the original edition were corrected, while excessive wordiness of the author was removed where it was thought to impede the reader's appreciation of his main points. However, Father Coleridge's writing style remains substantially unchanged. He was assigned to Immaculate Conception, better known as Farm Street Church, the flagship parish of the Jesuits of nineteenth-century London, located in the Diocese of Westminster.

Preface

The present volume embraces a distinct and separate stage in the history of the Incarnation. Our Lord's life in the womb of His Blessed Mother is a part of His infinite condescension which calls for a corresponding and particular devotion on our part. As the present volume reaches from the Annunciation itself to the eve of the Nativity, it covers the whole of this unborn life of Our Lord. It is enough for devout Christians that there exists this separate portion of Our Lord's human existence, the period of His greatest humiliation and self-abasement. It is only natural that this should at once attract our adoring homage and that those who give themselves to the special devotion which it suggests should find themselves consoled and assisted in a wonderful degree by the practices and contemplations which belong to that devotion.

There are many reasons for this devotion. In the first place, it sets before us the complete interior picture of the Sacred Humanity itself, the immense treasures which constitute that fullness of grace of which we all receive, and the intense activity of the heart and mind of our Lord when no other activity was possible to Him. It was a life almost entirely addressed to God and the object of His delight. Moreover, it was the true foundation of all that followed. On this account, we find those Christians who entirely ignore it generally wanting in an intelligence of the simplest truths of faith concerning the Incarnate Son of God. The Babe of Bethlehem is like any other child to them, as He was to the people of Bethlehem itself. The misconception leads to an inadequate idea of the whole life, office, and work of Our Lord: Who He is and what He came to do.

Again, Our Lord's Life, at this time, reveals the work and office which He at once gave Himself to discharge toward His Father. The created existence which began at the moment of the Incarnation was the greatest work of God. It may be considered as the crown and completion of the creation of the universe. Holy Scripture speaks of Our Lord as the head and consummation of the whole creation. He was sent indeed on earth for the redemption of mankind, and for their instruction in the manner of serving God perfectly, but as it is implied, His presence as Man added the crowning dignity to the creation as it was originally left. Only through Him could there be that perfect and worthy service to the Creator, which no one could give to Him but a Divine Person. God's greatness, beauty, and majesty, as displayed in the creation, required the most perfect appreciation, gratitude, and praise, and these had never been rendered to Him adequately, nor could they ever be so rendered, until the moment of the Incarnation. The life which then began paid this homage to the immense glory of God from the very beginning, in a thousand acts of adoration and self-abasement, oblation, and thanksgiving. The soul of Jesus Christ was a living mirror which gave back to God the perfect representation of His glories and wonders in an adoration of reverence, delight, and gratitude which was of infinite merit and worth, because it was the homage of a Divine Person.

Now at length God could be understood, thanked, and honored in an ineffably adequate manner, by a created intelligence and will united to a Divine Person, and that thus at last He could have from His creation a worship worthy of Himself. Our faith teaches us that it was this that was brought about by the Incarnation and that this work was complete from the very first instant of the Divine Union. This was the occupation and life of Our Lord during these nine months, when He did not begin as yet to redeem, or to atone, or to teach, in the ordinary way, as He did afterward, but when He began from the very first moment to devote Himself to honoring and glorifying His Father by the most intense acts of love and adoration. The eye of faith can see, in the circumstances of this stage of His Life, many holy and tender lessons of humility, obedience, silence, recollection, dependence, and other virtues. We may gather also that at the first moment of this adorable life was made the great oblation of Himself, to undergo all that had been decreed for Him to suffer in order to repair the sins of all the world before the justice of God. But the occupation of the Sacred Heart during these long months, an occupation never to cease for all eternity, was the employment of all His faculties of intelligence and affection upon the greatness and loveliness and majesty of God.

These nine months are the time in Our Lord's life which seems most entirely given up to this employment. God was all in all. Out of this life in the womb, which had no external manifestation at all, there sprang all the beauties and charities of the after stages of Our Lord's life. It is this life which continues now in heaven where He sits at the right hand of God, and in order that earth may not be without this continual and most perfect worship, He remains among us on the altar, not only to be the food and consolation of the devout souls who receive Him and live by Him, but also that from Him may rise up, day after day and night after night, as long as the world lasts, His own most loving adoration, most powerful intercession, and most intelligent praise. In the Blessed Sacrament, He lives indeed for us, but His life there is a return to His former existence in this stage of His infancy, only that He has added to it, in His infinite tenderness and most ingenious and long-suffering love, the marvelous communication of Himself which embodies all the choicest fruits of His life and passion.

We may understand in this sense also the words of Our Lord in His last prayer to His Father before the Passion, "I have glorified Thee upon earth, I have accomplished the work which Thou gavest Me to do, and now glorify Me, O Father, with Thyself with the glory which I had with Thee before the world was"[1]—that is, give to My Humanity the glory which belongs to Me as Thy Only-Begotten Son.

For the perfect glorification of the Father, of which Our Lord speaks, must certainly include the utter self-abasement with which He began, humbling Himself even to the condition of a babe in the womb of a woman, the nearest approach to utter annihilation of self that can be conceived, as well all

---

1 St. John xvii.

the other service and homage and obedience and praise and worship of which His life was made up as it advanced.

Another momentous fruit of an intelligent devotion to this part of the sacred infancy is the light which it throws on the position of the Blessed Mother of Our Lord in the kingdom of her divine Son, His dependence on her and union with her, the immensity of her graces and the supreme perfection of her virtues. His dependence on her as her child was different from that which is ordinary, on account of His full consciousness and perfect possession and use of all His faculties of intelligence and will. It is during this period of the nine months that He was hers and hers alone, and that she fulfilled the duties of the whole human race in regard of the honor and service due to Him. It is now that the pre-eminent greatness of the Mother of God seems to dwarf the magnificent perfections even of the highest of other saints, on account of her unapproachable nearness to Our Lord, her incomparable dignity as His Mother, and her unexampled faithfulness to the graces which she received, while all the time she is almost as hidden and silent as Our Lord Himself. Again, the devotion which is fed on the contemplations which belong to this stage of the history involves a constant exercise of the highest faith, and the devotion is rewarded by a great increase and deepening of that most precious virtue.

I trust that no one will blame me for having given so large a part of the present volume to an attempt to unfold the meaning of the two first Evangelical Canticles, especially the Canticle of our Blessed Lady. This may be considered as, in one sense, the first utterance of Our Lord Himself, as well as a revelation of the thoughts and affections of His

Blessed Mother which has no parallel at all in the rest of Sacred Scripture. The other chief subject contained in the present volume is the Preparation of St. Joseph for his high and peculiar office in the accomplishment of the decree of the Incarnation and all that followed on it.

H. J. C.
31, Farm Street, Berkeley Square:
Feast of St. Michael, Archangel, 1885

Chapter I

The Salutation of the Angel

St. Luke i. 26–28; Vita Vitæ Nostræ, § 4.

The sacred narrative tells us nothing as to the time or place at which the Annunciation occurred, except that it was at Nazareth. The words of St. Luke, about the angel entering in, seem to imply that it was in the house that the message was delivered. The apparitions of St. Gabriel in the Sacred Scriptures are more than once connected with the time of the offering of the evening sacrifice in the Temple, a time which may have been, to all the devout Jews, whether at Jerusalem or elsewhere, a time of adoration and prayer. It was at this time that St. Gabriel appeared to Daniel, and it was at this time that he had appeared in the Temple itself to the holy Zachary. Thus the devotion of the Church, which keeps the *Magnificat* of our Blessed Lady for the Vesper service, would have a kind of foundation in the history of the Annunciation.

All the details of the scene are veiled from us in the simple brevity of the Gospel words. But we are not forbidden to fill them up for ourselves out of the contemplations of the saints. We may well suppose that Mary was praying earnestly for the fulfillment of the promises made to the holy nation. They occupied her thoughts day and night: "I saw," she said to St. Bridget, "a star, but not such as shines from heaven, I saw a light, but not such as shines in this world. I perceived a sweet odor, wonderfully sweet and such as cannot be described. It filled everything, and I was exulting with joy on its account. And then immediately I heard a voice, but not from human mouth. On hearing it I was much afraid, thinking in myself, whether perchance it was an illusion. And immediately there appeared to me an Angel of God as a most beautiful man, but not clothed in human flesh."[1]

But it is time for us to give the simple words of the Evangelist, in which the history of the Annunciation is related, probably, from our Blessed Lady herself. St. Luke has just told us that St. Elizabeth hid herself for five months after the conception of her son. The narrative of the Annunciation is a continuation of the same record.

> And in the sixth month the Angel Gabriel was sent from God into a city of Galilee called Nazareth, to a Virgin espoused to a man whose name was Joseph, of the house of David, and the Virgin's name was Mary. And the Angel, being come in, said unto her, Hail, full of grace, the Lord is with thee, blessed art thou among women. Who having heard, was troubled at his saying, and thought within herself what manner of salutation this should be. And the Angel said to her,

---

1 St. Bridget, *Rev.* i. 10.

> Fear not, Mary, for thou hast found grace with God. Behold thou shalt conceive in thy womb, and shall bring forth a Son, and thou shalt call His Name Jesus. He shall be great, and shall be called the Son of the most High, and the Lord God shall give unto Him the throne of David His Father, and He shall reign in the house of Jacob for ever, and of His kingdom there shall be no end. And Mary said to the Angel, How shall this be done, because I know not man? And the Angel answering said to her, the Holy Ghost shall come upon thee, and the power of the most High shall overshadow thee, and therefore also the Holy One which shall be born of thee shall be called the Son of God. And behold, thy cousin Elizabeth, she also hath conceived a son in her old age, and this is the sixth month with her that is called barren, because no word shall be impossible with God. And Mary said, Behold the handmaid of the Lord, be it done to me according to thy word. And the Angel departed from her.

We must first consider the opening address of St. Gabriel to our Blessed Lady. "Hail, full of grace, the Lord is with thee, blessed art thou among women." The word *Hail* is the common salutation, wishing joy and happiness, implying respect and good will. The word which our version most rightly renders "full of grace" is applied somewhat in the same way as when we speak of persons being "graced" or "gifted." The words might have been rendered "Hail, graced one, or fully graced one," and the meaning would then have been conveyed that the person to whom the words were applied was endowed with grace in its fullness, that the process, so to say, of her endowment with grace was as complete as it could be. The words *gratia plena*, and our English words *full of grace* express the same meaning, while they convey most perfectly the theological truth also that grace is a quality or substance which is in the soul itself, not merely the favor with which the soul may be regarded, without any actual possession of the quality signified by the word.

The words of the angel imply, by their own force and weight, that the soul of Mary was at this moment already filled with grace. We have had to interpret the great words of St. John in the opening of his Gospel, in which he tells us that the Incarnate Word of God dwelt among us, full of grace and truth, and that of His fullness we have all received, and grace for grace.[2] The plenitude of grace, in the case of the blessed Mother of Our Lord, must be considered as the fullest and highest possible participation of the fullness of the grace of the Incarnate Word, although, the Incarnation had not yet taken place. But all the graces of Mary were for the sake of her Son, all given to her with the view of fitting her for the supreme honor of becoming His Mother. We may therefore speak of the graces of the sacred humanity of Our Lord, although they did not at this precise moment as yet exist. Those who have written on this great subject tell us that there are three kinds of plenitude of grace. The first is in God, in Whom alone are all good things, all gifts, all graces, essentially and infinitely perfect. God can receive no grace, for He is the one full and inexhaustible fountain of

---

2 St. John i. 16.

grace, a fountain which may give out countless treasures of the highest graces to His creatures, and which yet remains infinite and undiminished in its own fullness.

The next kind of fullness or plenitude is that which belongs to Christ as Man, the sacred humanity of Our Lord. It is this of which St. John speaks in the words just now quoted. It is of this fullness that we have all received. The fountain and source of all the graces of the sacred humanity is the union with the Divine Person of the Word of God, and it is from the One Godhead, which He possesses in common with the Father and the Holy Ghost, that Our Lord as Man receives infinitely and without measure, as the same Evangelist says, every kind of grace. As His grace is without measure, His works were all of infinite merit, all proceeding from infinite and most perfect charity, and by them He merited indeed, though not for Himself, but for us. Thus, indeed, He is full of grace; He has as Man by grace what He has as God by nature, and no grace in Him was ever wasted or idle. This is the fullness of grace which belongs to our Lord as Man.

These two great plenitudes of grace might be said to have been in Mary in a certain way, because she had within her, after the Incarnation, God Himself to Whom the first plenitude belongs, and Our Lord also as to His humanity, to Whom belongs the second. But speaking strictly, Mary cannot have either the fullness which is infinite and which sheds itself on all creatures without exhausting itself, nor can she have the imparted grace of the fullness which was in Our Lord as Man, in Him alone without measure. In the same way, she could not have been so full of grace as not to be able to receive more, or to increase in grace, nor, with regard to the fullness of truth of which St. John speaks, could she in her mortal life have had that in such a manner as to know all things, nor did she behold God as He is in the way in which the saints in glory behold Him. Her plenitude of grace was the plenitude of a pure creature, and therefore immeasurably distant from that which is in God and in Our Lord. When the angel addresses her as full of grace, he must be understood as implying that she was as full of grace as she could be full. And the saints and Fathers tell us that she was thus so full of grace as that she could have had no greater fullness unless she had been herself united to the Godhead, as was the humanity of her Son. The reason for this is the simple principle that she had been raised, or was to be raised, to a dignity than which no higher, under God, can possibly be conceived, the dignity of the Mother of God.

This kind of fullness of grace, flowing over, so to say, on all that is said or done by the person who possesses it, is thought to have been in the holy apostles and in others. But it must have been in our Blessed Lady in a higher degree than in any of the saints. Our Blessed Lady was far closer and more united to her divine Son than any of the saints could be, and therefore she must have received from Him the treasure of which we are speaking far more perfectly and largely than any other.

We must add a further thought. The graces of our Blessed Lady, wonderful as they were even at the very outset of her life, when the privilege of the Immaculate Conception was bestowed on her, were nevertheless always such as admitted of growth and increase. We believe that she did continually advance and increase in grace, from moment to moment, with a swiftness and ease and invariable continuity of growth of which there is no other instance in the whole creation, as her dignity as Mother of God has no parallel therein. It cannot be doubted that the continual growth of Mary in every grace was a special subject of delight to God, distinct from her simple possession of so many graces, and from her practice of the highest virtues, interior and exterior, from the moment when she became capable of such exercise of her gifts. But this peculiar beauty of the unfolding, before the eyes of God, of this most beautiful flower of paradise, is something which it is beyond our power to draw out in our present exile from heaven.

As the Holy Ghost is the Divine Person to Whom in a special manner is attributed the carrying out of the Incarnation, it is reasonable to suppose that His gifts were most fully and lavishly bestowed upon Mary from the very moment at which her soul became capable of receiving them, and that He ever afterward took a special delight in increasing them, in their beauty and efficacy. Indeed, short as the records are which remain to us, they seem not to be too short to show us the continual exercise of these gifts. It is indeed most important for us, in our considerations of the mysteries of the Incarnation, not to have any limited or jejune estimate of the amount of graces possessed from the very first by her, who was so chief an agent in them all. The gifts of the Holy Ghost are usually divided into two classes, according to the faculties of the soul which they affect and elevate and, as it were, transfigure, with new powers. Four of the gifts affect the intelligence. These are the gifts of wisdom, understanding, counsel, and knowledge. The remaining three, the gifts of fortitude, piety, and fear, perfect the will and make its action noble and lofty. In the possession of each of these classes of gifts our Blessed Lady was unique among pure creatures. As to the first, Mary was immensely nearer to God than anyone else could be; her charity, which was the uniting principle between Him and her, was such as to bind her closer to Him than any but she could be.

The just in this life are said to hunger and to thirst after God, and the blessed in heaven to be satiated with the possession of Him. This hunger and thirst on the one hand and this satisfaction on the other hand represent the two stages of the workings of this gift of wisdom in their souls. In our Blessed Lady, the result of this gift was something which raised her above the state of hunger and thirst, because she had the perfect cognizance of God in the sacred humanity of Our Lord, and yet she could not have as yet the full satiety with which her soul was to be flooded in heaven.

St. Antonine here quotes the Blessed Albert the Great concerning the gift of understanding as possessed by our Blessed Lady. He tells us that she had certain privileges of her own. She had by grace, even in this life, a very perfect knowledge of the Divine Trinity and, in the same way, of the mystery of the Incarnation, though in this case her own long familiarity with it and with Our Lord was, in part, the ground of her privilege.

The gift of counsel, according to St. Thomas, is that by which the Holy Ghost directs us in all things which are ordained to the end of our eternal life, whether they are commandments necessary to salvation or not. "But Mary was a most perfect observer, both of the commandments and of the counsels of God. She had beyond all, therefore, the knowledge of His counsels by this gift of counsel. She was also most dear to and familiar with God above all others, and so instructed even in the greatest secrets. Among the other counsels of God are poverty, virginity, and obedience, and she observed these in their highest perfection. She was most poor," as we see in her offering in the Temple. "She was the first to make the vow of virginity, which she always observed without the slightest contrary movement, and she was most obedient," as we see in the mystery of her purification, to which she was not bound, in her journey to Bethlehem, in her visit to Jerusalem, for the feasts and the like.

We pass over for the present what the saint tells us about the gifts of fortitude and knowledge. He makes the gift of piety consist in three acts: in disposition for works of mercy, in perfect obedience to the Sacred Scriptures, and in due honor to holy persons and things. He has little difficulty in showing the perfection of these acts in our Blessed Lady. She was moved to works of mercy by considering all men, not only as the images of God, but also as representing Him in a new way in consequence of the Incarnation. The simple words of the angel were enough for her to ground on them her stupendous act of faith, when she said, "Behold the handmaid of the Lord, be it done to me according to thy word." She was in her lifetime the pattern of veneration for all holy things and places, feasts and the like, and we probably owe to her the first example of the veneration which has always been shown in the Church to the special objects of Christian devotion, such as the Holy Cross, the

Holy Sepulchre, the Way of the Cross, relics, and the Blessed Sacrament.

Lastly, the saint comes to the holy gift of fear. There are, he says, three kinds of fear. There is the fear of servants, which consists in the apprehension of punishment for disobedience; there is the chaste fear, of which the Psalmist speaks,[3] and this has two acts, the fear of separation from God, like the fear of a pure spouse lest she should lose her beloved; and the fear of reverence, which consists in a very humble veneration, mixed with love of the thing or the person venerated. It was this last which was so excellent in Mary. She could not fear chastisement, being without sin, nor could she seriously fear to be separated from God, being confirmed in grace. But she was overwhelmed with the thought of the magnificence and greatness and mightiness and majesty of Him Who had lavished His choicest blessings on her and raised her to a height unparalleled among His creatures.

Lastly, he treats at considerable length what he calls her special privileges. These are in truth so many natural and reasonable deductions from her one fundamental grace of the divine maternity. It may be well summarily to mention them now.

The first privileges in this series are her perfect freedom from all sin, whether original or actual, mortal or venial, and even beyond this, the kind of impossibility of sinning in her which has been explained above. The saints in glory cannot sin, because they are absolutely united to God, in Whom there can be no sin. In this sense, Mary was not incapable

---

3 Psalm xviii.

of sin, because she was not as yet united to God in the state of glory. But she was united to Him by the plenitude of her grace, yet there was in her condition nothing at all that could bring about a separation from God, and in this sense, her plenitude of grace was incompatible with sin.

The next privilege was that she was the expression of the highest purity. The purity of which the saint speaks is not simply freedom from what is impure, but the closest possible approximation to the supreme purity which is in God, and to this privilege Our Lady attained by four stages, deriving greater and higher grace from the bounty of God. These four stages were, as St. Antonine tells us, her Immaculate Conception and the graces received therewith, her practice of virtue as her years went on, the coming on her of the Holy Ghost for the accomplishment of the Incarnation in her, and her Virginal Conception of the Son of God.

The next of the privileges of Mary was that she was at once Virgin and Mother. Both maternity and virginity have a kind of natural glory of their own. But in Mary, both were meritorious and deliberate, meritorious because so deliberate. Her virginity was the most perfect purity of mind and body, springing from her consummate charity and love of God, and her maternity was accepted and willed.

And her fruitful virginity and most pure maternity made her the Mother of God. Under this privilege is included the whole of her wonderful relations with Our Lord, from the moment when He became her Son in her most chaste womb, her interaction with Him during the nine months, the thirty years after His birth, and throughout all the ages which have since passed, throughout all eternity. This privilege has lasted on in ever increasing glory and magnificence, and will last on forever.

But if the maternity of Mary was thus a privilege which cannot be measured in its fruits and results, a privilege which is as fresh and fruitful in heaven at this moment as it was at the first instant of the Incarnation, so also is the virginity of Mary a privilege which lasts on and is continually most fruitful. For she is called in the litanies sung in her honor "Sancta Virgo Virginum," and she deserves this title on two accounts. In the first place, she was the first to discern the inappreciable treasure of holy virginity and to raise its honor in the world to the immense glory of God and benefit of mankind. And, in consequence, she is the mother of all holy virgins, a countless throng of both sexes, who have served God faithfully in this holy state. And in the second place, Mary is the virgin of virgins because she is the one most perfect and incomparable instance of virginity. For her virginity was not, as in others, a crown which had to be defended against the assaults of internal concupiscence, for in her the root of evil concupiscence was destroyed, and it was in itself of a purity which has no peer. It has also the unattainable glory of fertility, fertility of that unapproachable dignity which belongs to the fruitfulness which generates the Son of God in human nature.

It is thought by some theologians that the Incarnation might have been, even if Adam had not fallen, and that thus there might have been a divine maternity which would not have been that which made Mary the mother of the Savior of the world. Even in this case, it cannot be doubted that Our Lord would have been the head of the whole universe by virtue of His incarnation, and that all the elevation of which creatures might have been made partakers would have come from and through Him. If so, Mary would still have had that relationship to all those who are members of Our Lord and who are united with Him in the nature which He has assumed through and from her. It is essential that this thought should be included in the idea of her maternity, and our grasp of this truth is confirmed by the position which she occupies in the sacred scroll of prophecy, as the second Eve, by the truth that she was not an involuntary or unconscious instrument of the Incarnation.

St. Antonine tells us that she is the mother of all those who have a share in the new creation which has been the work of her Son. She bares Him for us, Who created us and regenerated us all by His passion, which confers the power of grace on the Sacraments, and she merited congruously by her virtues that she should bring forth Him as her Son. It was from her most pure flesh and blood that the Holy Ghost, by her own consent, took the flesh which He transformed into the Body by which our redemption and new creation were effected. Moreover, Our Lady, by her wonderfully godlike conversation, was to us the pattern and example of our turning away from darkness to light, and our perfect conversion unto the vision of the primeval light. And lastly, he says that the whole work of our redemption and new creation was ordered by God to her glory and honor. Thus the vision of the Apocalypse represents the elders in heaven casting their crowns down before the feet of the Lamb,[4] as if

4 Apoc. v. 8.

to acknowledge that they owe all to the humiliation of Our Lord and the sacred humanity which He took of Mary. And he says that this truth of the maternity of Mary over all who are redeemed by her Son is touched on in her own words in her Canticle, where she says that from henceforth all generations shall call her blessed. For the regeneration and re-creation of all things by means of the Incarnation make her in this sense the mother of all.

It is a part of the same truth that Mary is called the Gate of Heaven. It is the function of a gate that through it everything must pass which enters or comes forth from the city of which it is the gate. This name has sometimes been applied to the saints, as it is used in the Apocalypse of the Apostles, and it is sometimes applied to the holy cross. Its application to Mary represents the truth that we have through her the whole of the blessings which come to us by means of the Incarnation, because we have, through her, her Divine Son. It means also that as we all enter heaven through her Son, we enter heaven through her, whose Son He was. It is well known how some of the fathers and saints have insisted on the doctrine that all graces pass through the hands of Mary to us, by the special disposition of God, and it would not be easy to see how the denial of this truth can be altogether consistent with the true appreciation of the Incarnation.

The third privilege of this class in our Blessed Lady is that she is the queen and mother of mercy. Although so many of the great attributes of God are manifested in the Incarnation, still it is true to say that His mercy is therein manifested more than all others, and that it is, in itself, the greatest of all the manifestations of His mercy. St. Antonine tells us that there is glory in heaven alone, that there is grace on earth alone, but that in heaven, and even in hell, as well as on earth, there is always mercy. For the blessed in heaven are rewarded beyond their strict deserts, and the enemies of God in the place of torment are punished less than they deserve. The Incarnation was beyond everything else a work of mercy, and its effects reach throughout all the kingdom of God. Thus Our Lord is the embodiment of the divine mercy, and it is but right that Mary should have a great position in this kingdom of mercy, as she has so large a part in the administration of all that her Son has wrought. She is herself the greatest instance of His mercy, because she has received more than all others, she has a larger share in the benefits of His redemption than others, and from this it is only congruous to reason that she must have an immense share and power in turning His mercy on others by means of her intercession.

We must constantly remind ourselves, in considering these privileges of our Blessed Lady, that she was not an unconscious or involuntary instrument in the Incarnation, nor was she an unwilling victim of all the agony she had to undergo when she stood by the foot of the cross. She freely was made the mother of the Redeemer, and she freely gave Him up for us all on the cross. She had thus much to do with the carrying out of the divine mercy on the human race, and it is not a farfetched thought that she stands, and always stood, before God, as the representative of His counsel of mercy. Thus she is the queen of mercy, with a nobler right to the title than her famous prototype Esther, who obtained by pure favor, and the influence of the affection which she had inspired in the king, the pardon and deliverance of the whole nation to which she belonged. Mardochai told Esther that she might have been raised to the kingdom for that very purpose in the providence of God, that she might use her influence in the great need and danger of her nation.[5] In something of the same way, Mary may have been raised so high and granted so much power, with the especial design that she should always plead for mercy, even when the justice of God might well have its course, if it were not for her office of asking again and again for pardon for sinners.

There remain, according to St. Antonine, two more of these privileges of Mary to be considered in our present short view of this great subject. The first of these two is that to her was communicated the passion of Our Lord. He founds this statement on the common interpretation of the prophecy of holy Simeon, on the occasion of her purification, and he quotes St. John Damascene, who says that the pangs of childbirth, which she did not undergo at the Nativity, were reserved for her in the crucifixion of her Son. St. Antonine explains his meaning in this way. The privilege of the communication of the Passion implies two things, her faith in the Crucified as God and Man and the suffering which was occasioned by her sympathy for His sufferings. Our Lady was the only one who had both these in full measure, whose faith was entirely unshaken and unclouded, and whose compassion was intense to the fullest measure of intensity. Her Son, he says, desirous of giving her the reward involved in such a privilege, chose to communicate to her the merit of

---

5 Esther iv. 14.

His passion, that He might make her a sharer in the benefit of redemption, inasmuch as that as she had helped in the work of redemption by her compassion, she might also become the mother of all in the new creation resulting therefrom, and, as the whole world is under an immense debt to God for His passion, so also it might be the debtor of Our Lady for her compassion.

St. Antonine adds that it is said of Our Lord that He had in His passion the height of sorrow and the height of joy, sorrow in the sensitive part of His humanity, and joy in the intelligent part of the same humanity. So it is also true to say of Our Lady that she then had the extreme of compassion from His sorrow and the extreme of sympathy in His joy. Her soul regarded the death of her Son as the extreme of pain to its nature, and in this way, she felt the extreme of sorrow, and at the same time, she knew that that death was the remedy by which mankind was redeemed, and so she felt the highest joy. Again, her love for Our Lord is the measure of her sorrow at His sufferings, and as her love was in every way most intense, so also her sorrow for His sufferings was in every way most intense. This was the cause, then, of the immeasurable height of her sorrow, and at the same time, as she loved God and her neighbor in the highest degree, and as from the Passion was to come the immense glory of God and the immense advantage of her neighbor, the Passion was on this account the cause of the most intense joy to her.

The last of these twelve privileges of Our Lady is her exaltation above all creatures. Because Mary is above all creatures, she is therefore above the angels. The devout doctor, St. Antonine, applies to Our Lady the rule of Our Lord, that whosoever humbleth himself shall be exalted, and the more anyone humbles himself, the more he shall be exalted by God in the realms of bliss. As Mary was the humblest of all except her Son, so in heaven is she the highest of all after her Son. And so he concludes his chapter on the fullness of grace in Mary by saying that she was full of grace in four ways. First, she had all the graces, general and special, of all creatures in the highest degree. Secondly, she had those graces which other creatures had not. Thirdly, she had grace in so great a degree that a simple creature was not capable of more. Lastly, she had in herself the uncreated grace Himself, that is God.

They are all founded on the supreme grace which none but Mary can receive, the grace of the elevation to the Divine Maternity. Let us take the four first in the catalogue of St. Antonine, and we shall see that they are simple corollaries from the fact of the Divine Maternity in itself.

It stands to reason that the Mother of God could never be allowed to be stained by sin. They also included so large a dowry of graces and spiritual aids to the will and the intelligence that it was easy for them to conclude that our Blessed Lady was incapable of sin, not by the destruction of her liberty, but by the overwhelming abundance of her grace. And in the same way, the fourth privilege, that she is the highest expression and loftiest instance of all purity in the true sense of the word. It claims for her simply the highest grace that can be conferred. The absolute freedom from sin of every kind—original, actual, venial, and even every possible imperfection—is the beginning of this chain of graces, which is completed by the consummate purity of this final grace made as high and as fruitful as possible.

If these first privileges in the list given by St. Antonine are simply corollaries from the fundamental truth that our Blessed Lady is the Mother of God, the three which follow hang together as being connected with that great privilege of the manner of her maternity, according to which she was to be at once the most fruitful of mothers and the most pure and unsullied of virgins. It seems to the Christian intelligence impossible to conceive that Mary could have been a mother otherwise than by remaining perfectly a virgin, that anyone but God and herself should have any part in the generation of the Incarnate God. If this fundamental privilege be once understood, the other privileges follow almost as a matter of course—namely, that she was most truly and perfectly mother, and the mother of the divine Person Who took flesh in her, and, again, that she is preeminent among virgins, the virgin of virgins, as the Church calls her, having thus the perfection and unattainable grace of having as a mother God Himself for her Son, and as a virgin, the singular dignity of uniting this inconceivable fruitfulness with her virginity, of being the Mother of God.

The object of the Incarnation was the Redemption of the world. If Mary the Mother of God was raised so high in the favor of God in order that she might be fit to be the conscious and willing instrument of this great work of the Incarnation, it stands to reason that her influence and power with God, which of necessity correspond to her graciousness in His sight, must be exercised in favor of those for whom He became her Son, and that she must have the office of being the patroness and advocate of all those for whom He was to die. As Our Lord made Himself our Brother by taking flesh in her most pure womb, our relation to her as His brethren must be that of children, and thus the holiest and tenderest of ties that can exist between creatures, that of motherhood and sonship, binds us to her and her to us by a bond that nothing can sever. When she ceases to be the mother of Jesus Christ, she will cease to be our mother through Him.

From the same consideration of the object of the Incarnation which was carried out in her womb, we arrive at the reasonableness of the other two privileges mentioned by St. Antonine, that she is the Gate of Heaven and the Queen of Mercy. Heaven is opened to us by Our Lord, and Our Lord is what He is to us through her, and thus she is the Gate of Heaven by the decree of God which gave Him to us through His mother. Unless we are to make a stop in the divine mercies and draw a line where we see no line drawn by God, it is natural to think that she has an office connected with the distribution of all the graces which flow to us from her Son. We have said that the Incarnation itself is supremely and above everything the exhibition of the fullness of the infinite mercy of God. No doubt it displays His power, His wisdom, and a number of His other attributes, in a marvelous manner, but still it is preeminently the realm of the mercy of God. The Redemption that was wrought on the cross was exacted, so to say, by the justice of God, but the Incarnation, which is the field of the action of Mary, is pure mercy.

And thus we may understand the contemplations of those saints who speak of our Blessed Lady as having the special office of pleading, with all the intensity of her maternal intercession, the interests of mercy and of mercy alone, as representing, if we may so speak, the mercy of God and nothing else before His throne in heaven, not urging His justice or rousing His indignation against sinners. It is as if that original act of mercifulness, which made God conceive the design of the salvation of the world by the Son of Mary, were now enshrined in her, the purest and the most holy and the most powerful of creatures, using her influence in that royal way which becomes a queen, who has a right to the heart of the King, and has nothing to do with His vengeance but only with His compassionateness and clemency. In this sense, we rightly speak of her as the Queen of Mercy.

Thus it is impossible to suppose that Mary had not the fullest participation of the Passion of Our Lord which it was possible for her to have. It takes but a moment to write these few words, but it will take all the years of eternity for the illuminated minds and inflamed hearts of the blessed in heaven to comprehend their full meaning. And again, after this consideration of the reasonableness, or rather the necessity, of this privilege of the communication of the Passion to Mary.

She was full of grace, and the fullness of her grace was that she might receive fitly, if it could be so, the dignity of the divine maternity. And now, having made her fit to receive that ineffable dignity, God is with her for the accomplishment of His purpose in the Incarnation, and whatever belongs to that accomplishment, on His part, is an element of the special assistance to and presence with her which the great words, "the Lord is with thee," are intended to convey.

Chapter II

The Trouble of Mary

St. Luke i. 29. Vita Vitæ Nostræ, § 4.

What has already been said is enough to make it appear to us very probable that our Blessed Lady may have divined the meaning, or at least suspected the meaning, of the words of the angel, and have already, from the first, seen in them the full revelation, at least in germ, of the will of God as to her own elevation. The words of St. Gabriel which follow presently are the unfolding more clearly of that which is wrapped up in the original salutation. When he tells our Blessed Lady that she has found grace with God, he unfolds more fully the meaning of what he has already said in the words, the Lord is with thee. When he goes on to speak of her conceiving in her womb and bearing a Son Whose Name she is to call Jesus, he unfolds again what he has already hinted in the salutation by which he hailed her as the blessed among women. Thus it is very probable that Our Lady understood the salutation as containing in itself what might involve the great and unique privilege of the divine maternity, notwithstanding her own resolution and vow to remain forever a pure virgin. But as yet nothing had been said by the angel on this point, even in the most obscure way, unless it were contained in the simple title of blessed among women, inasmuch as the highest of all blessings of which women are capable is that of the most fruitful maternity united to most pure and unsullied virginity. This then may have been the effect of the salutation of the angel on the enlightened mind of the Blessed Virgin. It was a message of the highest dignity, speaking of the loftiest graces and the most wonderful elevation.

This may account for the next incident in the narrative, of which we are now to speak. This is the trouble of the Blessed Virgin at the words of the angel. "Who having heard, was troubled at his saying, and thought within herself what manner of salutation this should be." The trouble of Mary was occasioned by the words of the message and not by the appearance of the messenger. It is highly probable that our Blessed Lady was well accustomed to visits from the angels, and in any case it was one of her great privileges to have a marvelous knowledge and intelligence of the angelic creation, and a great discernment of spirits. Thus it is not likely that she would be simply frightened at the appearance of St. Gabriel, in the way in which St. Zachary had been frightened. It is therefore better to look elsewhere for the cause of the trouble of the Blessed Virgin of which the sacred narrative now tells us.

The great commentator Toletus shall explain to us the manner in which it seems right to understand this trouble. He begins by laying down for us the various kinds of trouble of which we find mention in the Gospels, for the sake of illustrating this passage. He takes in the first place the trouble of St. Zachary at the appearance of the angel to him in the Temple. In the second place, he puts this trouble of our Blessed Lady. In the third place, he speaks of the trouble of Our Lord Himself, of which mention is made in three separate places of the Gospel of St. John, once in the account of the raising of Lazarus, where it is said that "He troubled Himself," again in the next chapter, where we have the account of the Gentiles who wish to see Him, when Our Lord said "now is My soul troubled," and again in the history of the Last Supper, where He is said to have been troubled in spirit before He spoke about the treason of Judas.[1] In all these cases, whether in Our Lord, in Our Lady, or in St. Zachary, the trouble was not simply in the mind, but must have to some degree affected the body also, as is usual when mental trouble takes place.

The difference discernible between the effects of the trouble in these various cases is great. In the case of St. Zachary, we see that the trouble went so far as to disturb his mind, inasmuch as he was led to give in to a kind of doubt, even as to the truth of the angelic message which was delivered to him. The trouble which affected our Blessed Lady could not go so far as this. For all the movements and affections in our Blessed Lady were fully under the control of reason, they could not either lead her mind away or even rebel against its dominion. Even in the saints of God these affections can rise up against the rule of reason, as St. Paul speaks of the law in his members contrary to the law of his mind. In the case of the saints and servants of God, the grace of God supplies the

---

1 St. Luke i. 12. St. John xi. 33; xii. 27; xiii. 21.

power of quelling this rebellion. But in the Blessed Virgin, it was different, for it was one of her privileges that she had no such unreasonable affections or movements. Her mind and reason were not only not liable to be overpowered by them, but they could not even be assailed by them. The privilege of Our Lord went beyond this, for in Him every affection was voluntary and fully deliberate. This is indeed witnessed to by the language of St. John, who speaks of Him as troubling Himself, and thus whenever He felt trouble, or distress, or fear, or sadness or sorrow, it was because He chose at that time to admit such affections to His soul, and exactly as far as He chose to endure and have experience of them.

Of these three degrees, none were to be found in Our Lord. These passions or affections could not arise in Him without or against His will. They could not assail and rebel against reason, nor could they in any way overcome it. In Our Lady, they could neither assail the dominion of reason nor could they triumph over it. Just as we say that neither of them had any sin, though not from the same cause. And Toletus adds that he is inclined to this opinion, because the power which our passions and affections have, of outrunning reason and taking possession of us involuntarily, comes from the original sin which we all inherit, and from which our Blessed Lady was altogether free.

This then being the case in general with the movements and affections which passed over the soul of the Blessed Virgin, we must answer any questions which may arise concerning the trouble of which we are now told by the Evangelist in accordance with this general doctrine. Thus we may begin by saying that it is most highly probable, if not certain, that the trouble of which we now hear was a voluntary movement of her mind, acting under the command of reason, and occasioned by something that was contained, or which she felt might be contained, in the message of St. Gabriel. If we ask what this was, we can find at least two things in the message, or in what it implied, which may have been the cause of this voluntary trouble. The first would be that the message was beyond all doubt one that presaged her elevation to some very high dignity in the kingdom of God. But it is certain that the words of St. Gabriel foreshadowed some very high dignity for her to whom they were addressed, and this would be enough to alarm seriously the intense and most profound humility of the Blessed Virgin.

Another point as to which she might have been alarmed may have related to the purpose of her virginity. She was already a married wife, though by the great grace of God her spouse had the same holy resolution with herself, and there was no fear on her part that he could ever place any hindrance in the way of the perfect execution of her holy and cherished purpose. But she could not but know that the embassies of angels in the sacred history were frequently connected with the miraculous or marvelous births of children, designed for some high office in the kingdom of God, and perhaps the divine counsels might require on her part, as on the part of St. Joseph, the sacrifice of this purpose of immaculate purity.

These are the two points in the angelic message which may have struck our Blessed Lady with some kind of alarm and made her proceed to examine in her own thoughts, as the Evangelist tells us, what sort of salutation this might be.

It might almost be rendered, where this salutation could be from, to what class of salutations did it belong. These words of the sacred text seem to point to the magnificence of the language as a kind of shock to her intense humility, in the first instance, as furnishing her with the ground of her voluntary trouble and of her careful pondering of the words of the angel before making any answer on her own part. Thus the greatness of the blessing which seemed to be held out to her made her pause and consider it, in the interests of her own incomparable humility. On the other hand, her vow or purpose of virginity rose up as another reason for deliberation in the interests of her purity. No definite proposal had been made to her, no direct injunction had been given to her, and she was therefore left in her own intense prudence to ponder over the words, consider their full meaning, and then make her own blessed choice in accordance with the will of God as it might be declared to her. There is something here like that of which St. Paul speaks in our Blessed Lord Himself, that He did not snatch at and grasp a prey the dignity of His Divine Nature, but humbled Himself and made Himself low, being made obedient unto death even the death of the cross.[2] Thus this first response on the part of our Blessed Lady to the message as sent her by God, the response of silence and deliberation, was the most perfect choice which she could have made under the circumstances of her great probation.

---

2 Philipp. ii. 8.

Chapter III

The Son of David

St. Luke i. 30–33. Vita Vitæ Nostræ, § 4.

"And the Angel said to her, fear not, Mary, for thou hast found grace with God." The angel may have been divinely illuminated to understand the causes of the timidity of the Blessed Virgin, and he proceeds at once to remove them. The causes may have been two: her great humility and the plan of life in perfect virginity which she had resolved on for herself as her special service to God. Both of these causes are met by the assurance that she is not to fear, for she has found grace with God. For those who have found grace with God need not fear any elevation to which He may raise them in His divine counsels, seeing that, if He is with them, no work can be too great for them, no position too sublime. For those whom He exalts will always have His support in their exaltation as in their abasement. As Abraham was assured by his immense faith that God could fulfill his promises through Isaac at the very time that He gave him the command to sacrifice that same beloved son on Mount Moriah, so Mary might be assured by her far loftier faith that if she was to be a mother, it would still be without the slightest detriment to her virginity. For God Who could raise up Isaac from the dead, if so He had willed, is able also to give the grace of fecundity to a virgin, and to preserve the unsullied purity of a mother. Therefore, there is no need for fear.

She had found grace with God, the special grace required for the accomplishment in her of the mystery of the divine maternity, with the perfect preservation of her immaculate purity. God had accepted her beautiful offer of herself in the holy estate of continence, and whatever He might afterward ask her to do or to become would not be a violation of that which He had so graciously sanctioned, and with which He had been so well pleased.

Having thus calmed the trouble of which the Evangelist has spoken, the angel goes on to unfold to our Blessed Lady the particulars of the divine message committed to him. He does this in the language of prophecy.

The angel goes on to describe the greatness and other characteristics of the Child Who was to be born of Mary in language continually taken from the prophecies. The most direct reference in this passage seems to be to the great prophecy which is found in the 88th Psalm with reference to David, "I have found David My servant, with My holy oil I have anointed him. . . . He shall cry out to Me, Thou art My Father, my God and the support of my salvation. And I will make Him My first born, high above the kings of the earth. I will keep My mercy for him for ever, and My covenant faithful with him, and I will make His seed to endure for evermore, and his throne as the days of heaven."

"He shall be great, and shall be called the Son of the Most High, and the Lord God shall give unto Him the throne of David His Father, and He shall reign in the House of Jacob for ever, and of His kingdom there shall be no end."

The first words of the announcement with which we are concerned leave no doubt at all as to the office to which our Blessed Lady was now called. The dignity of the divine maternity may have been veiled in the earlier words, in which she was saluted as full of grace. For the fullness of grace was the appointed and legitimate preparation for the work of being the fit Mother of God. But what was before veiled and hinted and implied was now openly declared without any ambiguity or reserve.

The words before us seem to contain a direct allusion to the great prophecy of Isaias, and thus to suggest to our Blessed Lady that she was to be the virgin spoken of in that prophecy, which was, in truth, a confirmation and assertion, for the particular purpose of the encouragement and consolation of the house of David at that time, of the original promise made in paradise. The word "behold" seems to convey this allusion, and as the virgin spoken of by Isaias was to conceive and bear a Son, so our Blessed Lady is told that she is to conceive in her womb and bring forth a Son. The language is precise and may be considered as adopted for the purpose of making it clear that the conception spoken of was not to be a spiritual or figurative conception but a natural conception, in the ordinary way, in the womb and of the substance of His Blessed Mother, only without any share of man therein.

Our Lord is most truly the Son of Mary, and Mary is most truly the Mother of God. He did not even choose to become man as Eve was made out of a part of the substance of Adam, for in that case Mary would not have been His mother. He chose to be the Son of a woman, as St. Paul says, of the seed and lineage of David, and thus our Brother by the closest of ties. He chose to cleanse and sanctify by His own touch and presence all that had been corrupted by the fall of Adam, conception, childbirth, infancy, the miseries and weaknesses of our gradual growth, our years of helplessness. He chose to be as truly the Son of man by a true generation, as He is the Son of God by a true generation, and to win for us that adoption as the children of God which is connected in Sacred Scripture with His own condescension in truly and perfectly becoming a child of Adam. The greatness of His love for us required that He should humble Himself as far as was possible to all the lowliness of our natural condition. This would not have been His if He had not chosen to be an infant for nine months in His mother's womb and to undergo all the humiliations and restraints and dependencies of our childhood and youth.

Moreover, it was an essential feature that our Blessed Lady should be His mother in all the perfection of maternity, and this includes all that utmost intimacy of union between Him and her, and of dependence of Him on her, which is involved in her discharge toward Him of the full functions of His only parent in His infancy and childhood and ever after. She was to conceive Him, and bear Him, and nurse Him, and suckle Him, and watch over Him, and by this relationship be raised to the incommunicable honor and power which she possesses by right in His kingdom.

Her honor in heaven is ours also, because she is of our race and family. She has taken away the disgrace which clung to her sex, because through that sex sin began, as she has raised the fallen race to which she belongs. And her power also is for us, for the intercession of a mother must avail more with a Son than the prayers of all beside, and for this very reason she has been so highly exalted by God, that we might have all the power of her prayer on our side, winged by her intense love for our salvation, as that of those for whom the precious Blood of her Son was shed. All this is included in the words of the angel that she shall conceive in her womb and shall bring forth a Son.

And, as the crown to all that he has hitherto said, St. Gabriel adds that she shall call His Name Jesus. She could not have been ignorant of the depths of meaning contained in the Holy Name now mentioned to her, especially when it came as the crown and consummation of the great prediction now delivered. This Divine Son, Who was to be conceived in her womb and born in so marvelous a manner, Whose conception and birth were to be the fulfillment of the great promises of God made from the beginning, was to be called Jesus. Thus our Blessed Lady is at once assured that her Child is to be the long foretold and anxiously expected Savior of the whole world.

"He shall be great, and shall be called the Son of the Most High." The passage which thus begins is the description by the angel, in language chiefly taken from the prophetic writings, of the sacred humanity of Our Lord. He is the promised

Seed of the Woman, God made Man, great from all ages with the greatness and perfection of the Divine Nature, and great, from the moment of His conception, when His human existence in body and soul began, with the greatness belonging to Him by virtue of the hypostatic union. Thus we may divide the great truths concerning Our Lord's incarnation into two parts, the first of which is contained in the declaration of the angel now before us, while the second is conveyed in his answer to the question of our Blessed Lady herself of which we shall presently speak.

The first quality which the angel attributes to Our Lord is greatness. He was to be great on account of His Person, the Person of the Son of God in human nature. From this greatness of His Person flows the greatness of His sanctity and of His power. And moreover, His greatness belongs in a special manner to the perfect accomplishment of that work. His work involved the revelation of His Father and the declaration of the truths of salvation and faith by word of mouth, and thus He is great in word. No man ever spoke as He spoke, as was said of Him by those who were sent to apprehend Him. He was to teach the greatest and most sublime truths in the most efficacious and marvelous manner. Moreover, He was to confirm His words by works. In the first place, His works were to go before His words. That is, the example of every most perfect virtue which He taught was to be preceded by His most perfect practice of that virtue. In the second place, He was to confirm His words by showing the divine authority with which He spoke. "No man," said Nicodemus to Him, "can do the works which Thou doest, unless God be with Him."

Of these elements of greatness, the angel touches mainly on those which are sufficient to mark out Our Lord as the great subject of prophecy. In the first place, he says that He shall be called the Son of the Most High. For the foundation of the greatness of Our Lord in prophecy lay in the truth that He was to be the Incarnate Son of God, God made man. Thus the words of the angel seem to convey the same truth which is set forth by St. Paul in the opening of the Epistle to the Romans, where he says of Our Lord that He was the Son of God, made to Him of the seed of David according to the flesh, and predestinated to be the Son of God in power.

The next words of the angel speak especially of the kingship of Our Lord, a characteristic that sums up all the other excellencies predicted concerning Him. For He came not only to redeem the world, to open heaven, and to win for man the thrones therein, but to do this by the application of His merits and the carrying on of His work, age after age, by means of the Church, the kingdom which He was to found as the inheritance of the throne of David. "And the Lord God shall give unto Him the throne of David His Father, and He shall reign in the house of Jacob for ever, and of His kingdom there shall be no end."

It is said here that the Lord God shall give to Him the throne of His Father David, because it is as Man that Our Lord receives this kingly power, and whatever He has as Man He receives from the Father as His Lord and God. The kings, the ancestors of Our Lord, who succeeded one after the other to the throne of David, received it simply by the right of human inheritance, but Our Lord received it by virtue of a divine appointment. The throne of David had passed away from the eyes of men, for its power was gone after the captivity of Babylon. But it was revived for Our Lord by the providence of His Father and bestowed on Him in fuller right and power than ever it had been held before. For the rod was to spring up out of the root of Jesse, the trunk which had been cut down, was to become again productive, and send forth its shoot, the new kingdom was to be a sign to all people, and all nations were to serve it. As the Incarnate Son of God, He was by right King of the whole creation, which was all summed up in Him and made for Him. Again, the dominion over all things was given to Him as a gift from His Father, as St. John says that He knew that the Father had given all things into His hands.

Moreover, the Christian writers tell us that as Our Lord's titles to His kingdom were so far higher than those of any other sovereign, so also was His dominion and kingly power more complete and perfect than those of any other. For earthly sovereigns have no right to command their subjects as if they were slaves, the property of their masters, whereas Our Lord's dominion extends so far that there is no part or element in our body and soul which is not absolutely His. No earthly king is anything more than a delegate and a subordinate to God, whereas Our Lord is God Himself. As this royal dignity of Our Lord is grounded on the hypostatic union, it follows that He possessed it by right from the moment of that union. The wise kings who came from the East to adore Him in His cradle bore solemn witness to this as the burthen prophecy, and from time to time, Our Lord allowed His royal dignity to be disclosed, as in His entrance into Jerusalem on the day of Palms, and, even when He stood as a condemned prisoner before Pilate, He bore witness to this truth that He was a King. So His Father, in His providence, would not allow His title of King to be blotted out from the title on the cross. But He did not exercise His royal right or authority, ordinarily, while He was on earth, in order that He might suffer, and leave us the example of His humility. It was after His resurrection and ascension that the continual exercise of His royal power was to begin.

"And He shall reign in the house of Jacob for ever, and of His Kingdom there shall be no end." These words, few and short as they are, sufficiently indicate the universal extent and endless duration of the kingdom of Our Lord. The words "the House of Jacob" signify that it extends to the whole people of God, the true Israel, whereas the rule of the House of David, in the history of the holy nation, had been limited. It is not so to be with the Christian kingdom of Our Lord. It is to be universal in the extent of its dominion, embracing all peoples and nations and languages. It is to last upon earth as long as the world lasts, and, when the history of earth is closed, it is to continue throughout all eternity in heaven.

Chapter IV

"How Shall This Be Done?"

St. Luke i. 34—Vita Vitæ Nostræ, § 4.

The Angel Gabriel had proceeded with the utmost gentleness and prudence in his disclosure to the Blessed Virgin of the great office to which she was called by God. He had confined himself to the glories of the sacred humanity of Our Lord as set forth in Scripture. To one so enlightened as our Blessed Lady in the intelligence of the Scriptures and of the ways of God, it could not be a matter of doubt that the promised Child of the House of David was to be the Incarnate God Himself. But this had been implied, rather than openly stated in so many words, by the angel, except that he had said that her Child was to be called, and therefore to be, the Son of the Most High. Nothing had as yet been said by St. Gabriel concerning the conception by the Holy Ghost and the whole manner in which this divine birth was to be brought about. It may also be said with much truth that this part of the great mystery had not been spoken of prominently by the prophets themselves. It was also clear from the faith which had been in the world since the first promise made to our first parents in Eden that the Redeemer of the world must be more than man. In the same way, the virginal conception of the Divine Child was plain from the prophecy of Isaias and Jeremias.

Our Blessed Lady may have had an intelligence of the secrets of God of which we have no idea, because she was so singularly prevented and favored by His graces, both of the understanding and of the will. But the saints of God do not trust their own surmises or thoughts. Thus, even if the illuminated intelligence of Mary had been made acquainted, in some marvelous way, with the ineffable condescension by which the Holy Ghost was Himself to work out the mystery of the Incarnation, nothing had been said to her on this matter, and therefore it was left for her to enquire in her humble and most modest manner, how this thing was to de done? As to this, she was much in the same position as that in which her spouse St. Joseph was left, after the Incarnation, until the moment came for him to have the mystery, and his own office with respect to that mystery, revealed to him by a special vision from heaven. That he was so left was the essence of the trial to which he was put. We may trace something of the same kind in the divine dealings with Mary herself.

There had hitherto been one singular reticence in the words of St. Gabriel. In ordinary communications of the kind to which this belongs—namely, communications made with regard to the birth and conception of some saint of God—it had usually been said that the wife was to conceive and bear a son to the husband. We have seen how the thought of the hindrance which her virginal vow might possibly present to the carrying out of the mystery, may have been the cause of that fear of our Blessed Lady which had been removed by the last words of the angel. His words assuring her that she had found grace with God would have been equivalent, in her mind, to a promise that that which she feared as possible would not be. But nothing had been added as to the actual manner in which the divine counsel was to be brought to its accomplishment. Thus when the angel ceased speaking, Mary was left without further positive assurance, except that she had found grace with God and was to be the mother of the Messias. This great work might, perhaps, have been wrought in various ways by God, but there was as yet no distinct intimation what the particular way was to be which He would choose.

Thus we see that these words of our Blessed Lady do not in any way imply a doubt of the truth of the message which the angel had delivered to her. As it was to take place in herself, it was the most natural and right thing for her to ask for directions how to act. This might have been the case even if Mary had not had the virginal vow binding on her of which we have already spoken. But as this bond lay on her, it was only right and natural that she should refer to it and refer to it in such a way as to show that she considered that way at least to be excluded which would have involved a violation of her vow. She was precluded from becoming a mother in the ordinary way of women. We may well think that if she divined that the Mother of God must be a mother in some more sublime and heavenly manner than the rest of mothers, still she might be kept by her own deep humility from imagining that she could be raised so high as to conceive by the operation of the Holy Ghost.

Moreover, the words of Our Lady's question show her intense love for purity and her fixed resolution not willingly to sacrifice her virginal dignity, even for the sake of the blessing held out to her. The words show unmistakably that she was bound by an irrevocable tie. It is unreasonable to interpret the words as simply meaning that up to the time of the Annunciation, she had remained a pure virgin. They must signify that she was so to remain forever, and this by an obligation from which she could not free herself and from which she would not free herself if she could. Thus it is quite true to say, as is said by some of the Catholic commentators, that these words show us quite plainly that Our Lady remained as untouched after the birth of Our Lord as before.

This then seems to be the meaning of the words before us, in which Our Lady draws out from the messenger of God the great and most wonderful truth concerning the manner of the conception of her Divine Son. Instead of showing any incredulity or any hesitation as to the truth of the message which had been delivered to her, Our Lady shows, by her question, the strongest and most lively faith. Soon after this we find St. Elizabeth, speaking, no doubt, under divine guidance, calling Our Lady by the name which signifies this her singular and transcendent faith. "Blessed thou that didst believe!"—almost as if the saint had had in her mind the incredulity of which her own husband Zachary had been signally punished by the justice of God by a chastisement under which he was still suffering when his wife thus spoke.

And this again certainly shows us the character of the bond by which Mary was bound to virginity. If it had been only her own desire, or resolution, or purpose, the question would have been whether she was to carry out that intention or purpose. She could not plead the difficulty which she does plead, unless she had been certain that what God had inspired He would not call on her to sacrifice, and that His will could not be the violation of the solemn vow by which she was to remain a virgin forever.

She was before all things the handmaid and servant of her God and Lord, and whatever choice she might make, or whatever desire she might conceive, was made or conceived, out of regard to His supreme will and out of obedience to Him. Her heroic faith made it easy for her to believe that He would find a way of His own for the accomplishment of both of His decrees concerning her, just as the faith of Abraham made it easy for him to think that God could still give him the promised seed in his son Isaac, even though He commanded him to offer him in sacrifice on the mountain. It was not to Abraham a choice between foregoing the promises which had been made to Him and disobeying the command to slay Isaac. He believed that what God had promised He was able to perform. So with Mary, she could believe as Abraham believed, though the thing which she had to believe was the more difficult of the two.

Our Blessed Lady could believe that if God willed her to be the mother of the Incarnate Word, He could and would provide some way by which this purpose of His could be brought to its full execution, without the necessity of her sacrificing that which she had promised to Him to maintain. But it is natural to suppose that her virginal purpose was very dear to her. It was the choice she was inspired to make, the first of all the servants and children of God. It was her treasure, as it were, her discovery under the guidance of the

Holy Ghost, like the treasure in the parable, her darling plan for her life, her glory.

And again, if the question of our Blessed Lady was so perfectly prudent, so full of faith and love, displaying so entire a submission to the Will of God, and so lofty an intelligence of His ways and of His power, it was also, as we shall see, most fruitful, in the great revelation to which it led. It was the key which unlocked the secret treasures of God and brought to light the ineffable condescension which He was preparing for the carrying out of the promise of the Incarnation. It has already been said that this part of the great counsel of God had not been as yet revealed. It was not told to prophet or seer, nor had it been written in the pages of revelation, nor divined by the contemplations of the saints. It was naturally reserved for the Blessed Mother herself to know first how the Incarnation was to come about. There was something wanting in the fullness of this great revelation until Mary unlocked this, its last treasure. It was not known before the time. When the moment came for the chosen virgin to ask this question, .then at last the final word was spoken by the mouth of Gabriel, and the angels who hung around him in eager expectation might rejoice over this clear manifestation in its minutest details of the beautiful design on which their contemplations had so long fed with ecstatic delight. "How shall this be done, seeing that I know not man?" The future queen of heaven and earth, the humblest and most docile of God's creatures, whose will was so entirely His that the slightest intimation of His desire was her law, was thus the appointed person to bring out, by her question, the mystery concealed from the foundation of the world.

Chapter V

THE CONCEPTION BY THE HOLY GHOST

St. Luke i. 38. Vita Vitæ Nostræ, § 4.

It has been said that the faith of the Blessed Virgin had already soared so high as to find no difficulty in the great announcement which had been made to her by the angel, while she had most prudently enquired what was to be the manner in which the mystery was to be carried out. The answer which the angel was now to give her was to rise to the full height of the most marvelous of the works of God, the conception of Our Lord in her womb by means of the operation of the Holy Ghost. Thus it could not but involve a fresh demand on her incomparable faith, a demand to which she was enabled by the grace of God to respond with the same perfect docility and ready intelligence as in the former case. We live on the mystery of the Incarnation, and we are so familiar with its details as they are set before us by the teaching of the Church that we do not comprehend the immense act of faith which was now required of Mary and which was made by her, as it seems, without any strain or effort.

The long history of the Christian Church informs us of the many various devices which have been adopted by those who have not been made able to receive the great truth, even after it has been made certain by divine revelation. Some of the heresies on the subject of the Person of Our Lord are very grotesque, while others show us how the human mind shrinks back from the full apprehension of so wonderful a truth as that of the Incarnation carried out as it actually was. We see the malignity of Satan in the many attempts made by the heresiarchs to pare down the divine truth so as to deprive man of the full benefit of the infinite condescension of his God. But we may also see, in the same false systems, the perversity of the human mind taking refuge in any imagination which may give it an excuse for not believing that God has done for us all that He has done.

Thus, in every imaginable way, the great mystery has been cut down and explained away. And it is very probable that outside the Catholic Church, this process is still constantly gone through in the minds of thousands who consider themselves Christians, mainly on account of the feebleness of the human mind to grasp the full truth, because it is so great and magnificent and complete on the part of God. It must be remembered that many of the ways in which heretics have supposed the union to have taken place, may have been in themselves possible if God had so chosen, though they would not have brought about an Incarnation in the true Christian sense of the word. They would not have given to us a Savior in the sense of the prophecies and promises of

God from the beginning of time. The full truth was now conveyed to the chosen mother by the next words of the angel, without any reticence or concealment, as to one whose faith could not be too severely taxed by the magnificence of what she was asked to believe on his simple word. "And the Angel said to her, the Holy Ghost shall come upon thee, and the power of the Most High shall overshadow thee, and therefore also the Holy which shall be born of thee shall be called the Son of God." Our Blessed Lady's own words had already excluded the possibility of the ordinary mode of conception in this case, and the angel seems to take her words up, and to supply what she could not have known without the special revelation now made to her, that the Conception was to be brought about by the action of the Holy Ghost Himself. She was to conceive as a pure virgin, but not by any simple act of her own will alone, for the Holy Ghost was to bring about the formation of the body of her Child from her most pure flesh. She was to be the sole parent of the Child, but the Conception was to be the work of the Holy Ghost. This is the great mystery which we must now endeavor to explain in accordance with the Catholic teaching on the subject of the Incarnation.

In the first place, some of the commentators insist upon the word used in the Gospel before us, *superveniet*, translated as "shall come upon thee." These writers suppose the word to signify that the Holy Ghost would come to Our Lady in a new manner, having been already with her, as He was certainly with her in the plenitude of His graces. This doctrine is perfectly true. He will come to her in a new and special manner for the purpose of bringing about in her, without the intervention of man, the miraculous conception of her Divine Son.

This then is the meaning of the coming of the Holy Ghost to our Blessed Lady. He is to come to her, for the purpose of accomplishing in her the work of the conception of her Son, and of fitting her for the part which she herself was to have in that conception. In the first place, the Holy Ghost was to come to her, to confer on her a new and great increase of sanctity, that she might be fit to give of her substance so that the sacred Body of Our Lord might be formed.

In the first place, then, it is undoubted that Our Lady was already full of grace, but this did not exclude the special action of the Holy Ghost for this particular purpose. He was to come upon her with a fresh abundance of graces and gifts, now that the message of the angel had been delivered to her so far, and she had so far corresponded in perfect faith and ready docility and obedience to the designs of God. He was now to dispose her finally, by His sanctifying power, that she might be worthy to conceive the Son of God, and that He might fully sanctify that body of hers from which was to be taken the substance of the flesh which was to be that of the Incarnate Word. This is that operation of the Holy Ghost of which the Church constantly sings when she prays to Almighty God, "Who with the cooperation of the Holy Ghost didst prepare the body and soul of the glorious Virgin, that she might merit to be made the dwelling place of Thy Son." This fresh and final sanctification of Our Lady, in body and soul, is the first effect to be produced by the coming upon her of the Holy Ghost of which the angel speaks.

The reasons which have been given sufficiently explain why the conception of Our Lord in the womb of His mother is a divine work specially attributed to the Holy Ghost, although all the works of God outside Himself are the works of all Three Divine Persons equally. The reason is because this conception of Our Lord had so much of the character of sanctification, not only in that the Holy Ghost formed and prepared, and brought about the animation of, the body of Our Lord, but also because He exercised His special function and office of sanctification by His operation in preparing our Blessed Lady, body and soul, for this Conception and by making the Conception itself intrinsically holy. Another reason is also given for this attribution—namely, that the gift of the Incarnation of the Son of God was something entirely gratuitous and unmerited by man, a pure act of the most infinite mercy. Now the gifts of God of this kind are usually in Sacred Scripture attributed to the Holy Ghost. Moreover, the end and object of this Conception was the sanctification of the whole world, and this is a work which especially belongs to the Holy Ghost.

The angel next goes on to complete his message. He has spoken of the action of the Holy Ghost in the sanctification of our Blessed Lady for the special purpose of her conception, and in the preparation and animation of the substance which was to become the Body of Our Lord. But this work might have been conceivably done with a view to the Conception of someone who was not in Himself divine, whereas in the conception of Our Lord, there were further mysteries and marvels to take place beyond this action of the Holy Ghost, limited as it might possibly have been to a merely human birth. The Child Who was to be conceived in the womb of Mary was indeed to have a perfect human nature, but He was to be at the same time a Divine Person. He was to have no personality or subsistence except a divine personality. For this it was necessary, in the designs of God, that the Person of the Word should be united to the human body formed in the womb of Mary and to the soul created and infused into that body by God, and that the Child should thus be at once God and Man, "God of the substance of the Father, Begotten before the worlds, and Man of the substance of His Mother born in the world." The words of the angel of which we have already spoken, "The Holy Ghost shall come upon thee," describe the formation of the human Body out of the substance of Mary, and out of her substance alone, and also the preparation of that Body for the reception of the Soul created by God for it. The words which follow describe the divine operation by which the Person of the Son of God was to be united at the instant of the Conception to the human nature, the Body and the Soul thus prepared for this ineffable union. And thus they complete the description of the Incarnation, in the fewest and simplest terms, making indeed a great demand on the wonderful faith of the Blessed Mother, but still not a demand too great for that stupendous faith.

The whole of the great mystery was carried out instantaneously, and in the same moment of time, and thus it is that the human nature of Our Lord had never for one moment a personality of its own, distinct from that of the Son of God. This truth is necessary for the intelligence alike of the mystery of the Incarnation, of the personality of Our Lord, and of the divine maternity of Mary. In the formation of the Body of Our Lord, our Blessed Lady had her part as mother, contributing of her most pure blood for the substance necessary for that purpose. The creation and infusion of the Soul was the work of God the Creator alone, in this case as in all others. The union of the Person of the Word to the human nature and, like the other works of the Ever Blessed Trinity was wrought by all Three Persons equally and in common. But, as it is a work of the most stupendous and marvelous power, it is one of those divine works which are particularly attributed to the Eternal Father.

This, then, is the meaning of these words, "the power of the Most High shall overshadow thee." The Eternal Father is spoken of as figuratively overshadowing the Blessed Mother, that she may become the mother of His Son, covering her with His infinite power that so great a Conception may take place in her womb as that of His own Only-Begotten Son, Whose sole parent, in His Divine Nature and Person He, the Father, is. And thus the Three Divine Persons have each one His proper work in the execution of the mystery. The Father works the work of power in the union of the Person of His Son to the human nature, the Holy Ghost works the work of goodness, beneficence, mercy, and sanctification in the preparation of that human nature, and the Divine Son Himself becomes Incarnate, and takes to Himself, forever and forever, the human nature, the Body and the Soul conceived in the womb of Mary.

"And therefore also the Holy which shall be born in thee shall be called the Son of God." These words form the conclusion of the direct message in which the mystery of the

Incarnation is explained to the Blessed Mother. The angel tells her that because of the two truths which he has revealed to her, the operation of the Holy Ghost in the first place and the Hypostatic Union wrought by the power of the Father in the second place, the Child conceived and to be born of her shall be the Son of God. But each word has its own weight and importance and must be considered singly. That which is to be born of Mary is in the first place Holy. Because of the operation of the Father, which the angel has spoken of in the second place, the Holy that is born of Mary shall be called the Son of God, not therefore simply a holy birth, by reason of the preparation of the Holy Ghost, but a Divine Person, by reason of the operation of the Eternal Father bringing about the hypostatic union. Thus what was already holy, for the reason so often mentioned, was to be holy with the particular and ineffable holiness of the Son of God, by virtue of this union.

What the angel had in charge to announce to St. Joseph was that He had been conceived by the operation of the Holy Ghost. In this place St. Gabriel seems to mean to imply that Our Lord was to be perfectly and completely the Son of His mother, and her Son alone, and not the Son of any earthly father, and that His substance was to be from her and of her, not a phantasm, or a substance taken from some other being, but really and truly hers. This was the effect of the operation of the Holy Ghost, while as the effect of the hypostatic union, which is attributed to God the Father for the reason already given, He was really and truly the Son of God even in His human nature. Thus, even apart from the hypostatic union, the conception of Our Lord differed from every other conception, however holy. Let us explain this a little further.

St. John Baptist was to be born holy from his mother's womb, but he had been conceived in sin, and his sanctification came after his conception. In the case of the immaculate conception of our Blessed Lady, she was conceived holy and Immaculate, entirely free from all taint of sin. But the act of her conception on the part of her parents was in the ordinary way, however highly sanctified by right intention and freedom from lust on their part. She might have been conceived in original sin, but for the intervention of the privilege of exemption accorded to her as the future mother of Our Lord, and for His merits. In this sense it is that she was conceived Immaculate. But Our Lord could not have been conceived in any sense in sin, for the reasons already given, and thus the angel speaks of Him in these words as the Holy, or the Holy One, Who is to be born in Mary. He was holy, with the infinite holiness of His divine nature from all eternity, and, by virtue of the union, His humanity also received the "anointing" of which Scripture speaks in more than one place, that is the holiness of God. And again His humanity was enriched with the plenitude of grace, with all wisdom and grace of the Holy Ghost. Both these sanctities the humanity of Christ had from the first instant of His conception, and thus He was in the strictest and fullest sense of the words, the Holy One.

Again, with regard to the title of the Son of God, this belonged to Our Lord both as God and as Man. He was of the same substance with the Father and possessed with Him the fullness of the divinity. His power and might were the same with those of His Father, and as He did not become the Son of God at His human conception, the angel says that He shall be so called, rather than that He should become. And He is said to be called the Son of the most High on another ground also because He is to be manifested as such to the world and to be honored and worshipped as such by the faithful. As Man He is the Son of God but by virtue of the hypostatic union. His humanity received thereby the natural filiation to God because it pleased God to communicate to it the eternal hypostasis of His Son, and in that His own divinity. Thus the filiation or Sonship of Our Lord to His Father is one, both as God and as Man, but He is the Son of God from all eternity as God, and as Man He is the Son of God by virtue of the union which took place in time.

It has been thought, for instance, by some heretics, that Our Lord was born a simple man from His mother's womb, and that afterward He merited or received the grace of the Divine Sonship. Other heretics taught that He received it at a much later period, when He was baptized by St. John, and the voice from heaven was heard, declaring Him to be the well-beloved Son, and the like. The graces and merits of the sacred humanity were themselves the effects and fruits of the divine union.

Our Blessed Lady had not questioned the possibility of the mystery which had been announced to her. She had only enquired how the mystery was to be carried out, especially as she was bound to remain forever a virgin. Though she had not asked for a sign of the certainty, it was due in the counsels of Providence that she should have a sign given her, by way of confirmation of the truth which had been revealed to her. Thus it was natural that some confirmation of the words of the angel should be given to Mary, though she neither asked nor required such confirmation for her own sublime and perfect faith.

Again, the conception of Our Lord in the womb of His mother had long been a subject of anticipation in the constant repetition in the sacred history of the incident of the marvelous conceptions of children by aged parents, when, in the course of nature such conception was either impossible or extremely improbable. If God had condescended to prepare the marvel of the Incarnation by such anticipations, it seems only right and orderly that when the Incarnation was to take place, it should be heralded by a fresh marvel of the same kind as before, as furnishing the crown and putting the finish to the long series of such providential anticipations. And another reason existed for the communication to Our Lady of the state of pregnancy of her cousin Elizabeth—namely, that it was the design of God to bring about the visit of Our Lady to St. Elizabeth without delay.

"And behold thy cousin Elizabeth, she also hath conceived a son in her old age, and this is the sixth month with her that is called barren, because no word shall be impossible with God." Every word of this short sentence is full of meaning. The truth of the message is confirmed by the fact itself of the marvelous conception of St. Elizabeth in her old age. She must have been well-known to Mary, and so her sterility and advanced age could not be a secret to her. She is spoken of as "her that is called barren," as if to imply that her sterility was well-known and a matter of common reproach to her on the part of enemies, and of sorrow on the part of friends.

The mention by the blessed angel of the state in which St. Elizabeth was would naturally suggest to Our Lady, even on the simple grounds of charity and kindness, that she should go to be of service to her under such circumstances. But there were higher grounds for her visit than those. It was implied by the angel that there was something marvelous not only in the conception of the child of Elizabeth but also in his destination and in the office he might have to discharge in the kingdom of God. It would have been easy for Mary to see that the child might have some task to perform in connection with that great deliverance of the people and the world which was the purpose of the Incarnation itself.

And still further, these words of the angel may have implied a kind of answer to any thoughts which might have arisen in Mary as to the immediate future. Her first thought might naturally be whether she was to reveal to her holy husband the mystery which was to take place. For what could she desire more than to make St. Joseph the partner of her great joy! And the words of the angel come as a direction to her rather to go to the home of St. Elizabeth, in the first instance, and there await further guidance from God.

The last words, "no word shall be impossible with God," are taken from the passage in Genesis in which the conception of Isaac is foretold to Abraham and Sara. This was the first in the line of similar anticipations of the supreme miracle of the conception of Our Lord, as the conception of St. John Baptist by Elizabeth was the last. Thus the words may be considered as summing up for our Blessed Lady the whole of this kind of evidence as prepared by God. And thus the full scriptural evidence on which Our Lady might build up her act of faith in the mystery now proposed was completed by the addition of the new marvel lately worked in the womb of her cousin.

The Blessed Virgin was illuminated in the ways of God beyond all others. The words of the angel are simple and short, and they must have set before Our Lady's mind the full height and stupendous wonderfulness of the Incarnation. Mary was thus asked to believe that she was to become the mother of God Himself by the operation of each Person of the Blessed Trinity. It might have been comparatively easy for her to understand that the prophecies with which she was so familiar, all pointed to the divine character of the Messias Who was expected. It might not be so difficult to believe that His mother was to be a pure and unsullied virgin. But it was something more difficult to nature to grasp, at once and without hesitation, that she was herself to be the chosen mother, the virgin who was to conceive and bear a Son. It is one thing to believe such a mystery at a distance and as a matter of prophecy, and another to rise in a moment to the truth that it was to take place in herself, in her own person, in her own womb, then and there. Mary could understand in this nothing short of the full truth, that the Divine Person of the Son of God was to take flesh of her.

In all these ineffable wonders, as Mary knew, "no thing was impossible to God." It was within His power that the Incarnation should take place in the way described in the words of the angel. It was within His power that a maiden of earthly strain should thus become a mother by the direct action of the Holy Ghost and of the Eternal Father, that the Only-Begotten Son of God should make Himself her child in her womb in the manner implied by these words. But then again, that she was to be the mother of God herself, she and no other, she the humblest of the humble, the lowliest of the lowly! Surely there was need here for a faith more ready, more sublime, more perfect than that of Abraham himself, the father of the faithful, when he was called on to believe that he was to be made the father of many nations, or again that his seed should be as the stars of heaven, or the sand by the seashore, and yet was told to offer the son in whom these promises were enshrined in sacrifice on the mountain.

St. Paul justly indeed celebrates this faith of Abraham as the pattern and model of all faith, whether in Jews or Christians. "He was not weak in faith," he says, " neither did he consider his own body now dead, whereas he was almost a hundred years old, nor the dead womb of Sara. In the promise also of God he staggered not by distrust, but was strengthened by faith, giving glory to God, most fully knowing that whatsoever He has promised He is able also to perform." And of the other great trial of Abraham, the Apostle says, "By faith Abraham, when he was tried, offered Isaac and he that had received the promises, offered up his only begotten son, to whom it was said, in Isaac shall thy seed be called, accounting that God is able to raise up even from the dead."[1]

The Incarnation towers so far above all the other great works of God as that nothing is really great in comparison. But it is a part of the same truth that the faith required to grasp at once and assent firmly to the revelation of the

---

1 Rom. iv. 18–21. Heb. xi. 17–19.

Incarnation, in all its wonderful details, must be a faith far greater than any faith that had ever been exercised by any creature up to that time, or that could ever be exercised again.

Yet this was what constituted the trial of Mary. She was asked to assent in her mind to the truth as it was now set before her, and also to consent with her free will to be made the deliberate and conscious instrument of this awful mystery. If faith is the condition of pleasing God, it must surely be a self-evident truth that the act of faith now required of Mary was absolutely unique in its greatness, and therefore such as to make her pleasing and acceptable to God in a degree to which there can possibly be no parallel.

Thus if we had no more knowledge of our Blessed Lady than that which is contained for us in this simple narrative of the Annunciation, we should have enough to justify all the most glowing language concerning her greatness in dignity and in grace that has ever been used by those among the saints and writers of the Church who have been most distinguished in their praises of her. The immensity of her grace and of her merit before God is shown by the fact that she was asked to give to the words of the angel a faith so stupendous that she did not fail in the trial to which she was thus subjected. It remains to see how the chosen instrument corresponded to the strain put upon her, and to the demand made on her faith and obedience.

Chapter VI

THE FIAT OF MARY

St. Luke i. 38. Vita Vitæ Nostræ, § 4.

The blessed angel had done his part. He had delivered his message in a few words, and now heaven and earth, God and man, and the whole creation which was to be ennobled and elevated and purified and renovated by the Incarnation, waited for the answer of the humble virgin of Nazareth. There was no delay, no hesitation, no half consent, God had said at the beginning, "Let light be, and light was." So now the word which was to bring about the accomplishment of the greatest of the designs and works of God followed instantaneously on the invitation of God that it should be spoken. Her ready answer, without any further questioning as to the manner in which the great work was to be wrought in her, shows sufficiently that there was nothing in the announcement of the angel which was a difficulty to her faith.

Gabriel had spoken three times. First, he had saluted Our Lady with words of the most magnificent import. She had said nothing, revolving first in her own most prudent mind what might be the meaning of so great a salutation. Her humility looked up plaintively to God for help through His angel. Then Gabriel had spoken again. His second words had conveyed an assurance that her humility would be aided by all the might of God, that she need not fear on the score of her virginal purpose, while they had also made it most clear that she was invited to be the mother of the promised Messias. Our Lady answered this great announcement by a calm and simple question as to the manner of the execution of the mystery. Then Gabriel had spoken the third time, and his words this time had risen above the loftiest flights even of the prophetic choir, and he proposed to her faith the whole wonderful design of the Conception in her virginal womb of the Eternal Son of the Father by the operation of the Holy Ghost.

We have already spoken of the answers or of the silence of Mary in regard to these three sentences of the angel. It may be said that her words now, short as they are, furnish a complete and most characteristic answer to all three speeches of the angel. He hailed her as full of grace, as having the Lord with her in a special manner, and as the blessed one among women. These words, to one so enlightened as Mary, could not have conveyed less than the intimation that she was the chosen mother of the Messias, the Woman spoken of in the first revelation in paradise, the virgin who was to conceive and bear a Son in the prophecy of Isaias. She now answers in her own perfect way. She does not speak as the chosen among women, as the royal virgin of the house of David, as the blessed one, between whom and Satan enmities have been placed by God. She speaks of herself in the way in which she delighted to think of herself, as the handmaid, the servant, the slave, of the Lord.

The words imply her perfect submission, her delight in doing whatever her Lord might require of her. In those words she at once expresses her faith, her intelligence of the meaning of the mystery in which she was called to bear her part, and the principle of her conduct, that of obedience to God as her Lord and Master. When she adds, "be it done to me," she gives her assent and obedience to the particulars of the command that she was to conceive in her womb and bear a Son Who was to be called Jesus. And when she adds the words, "according to thy word," she implies the most perfect faith in the great wonders of her conception, while at the same time she speaks with the most refined humility, not mentioning or dwelling upon these magnificent works of God which were to raise herself so high.

Thus every word in this last answer of our Blessed Lady is the manifestation of some high virtue. Her readiness and joyousness in making herself the instrument of the designs of God are shown by the first word, "Behold!" Her profound humility reveals itself in the term by which she speaks of herself as the handmaid of the Lord. The words "be it done to me" show her marvelous faith. For the angel had not said she was to do this or that, but that the Holy Ghost should come upon her and the power of the Most High should overshadow her. And the last words "according to thy word" show her faith and humility, as has been said, as also her joy that the accomplishment of the work was to be brought about in the manner which increased instead of diminishing or impairing the glory of her chastity.

The same words must also be understood as gathering up in themselves all the intense desires with which this Blessed Mother had looked forward to and longed and prayed for, the accomplishment of the Incarnation for which she had yearned and longed more ardently than all the old prophets and saints from the beginning of time. Indeed she seems to speak, not in her own name only, but in the name of the whole race of which she was the representative in the Incarnation, because God and man were to be united in her womb and by means of her. She speaks in the name of the whole creation, for the whole creation was to be raised to union with its Creator by the mystery to which she now gave her consent. Her *fiat* is the prayer of all the world, rising up with the final and ineffable efficacy which was to prevail and win the greatest mercy of which even God is capable toward His creatures. St. Paul tells us that the whole creation groans and is in labor for the revelation of the Sons of God. And now Mary seems to stand between God and His creatures, the highest of all as yet existing, because the One Who is infinitely higher than Mary was not yet conceived. And she raises her humble voice to the throne of God and says, "Let it be as Thine Angel has said!"

"And the Angel departed from her." His work was done with the conclusion of his embassy and the consent of the Blessed Virgin, and it was fitting that she should be left alone with her God that the work of the Incarnation might be wrought in her by Him.

The theological writers, who have treated of the subject of the great graces bestowed upon our Blessed Lady, usually consider that at the moment of the conception of her Divine

Son, she was adorned by God with a new and immense dowry of graces. The whole history of created sanctity can contain no instance in which the human soul manifested higher and more perfectly beautiful perfection. For the act of the Incarnation was the greatest act of the divine mercy and condescension possible. It was the fulfillment of the loftiest and most far reaching of the counsels of God. It was the elevation of the whole creation by its union with the Creator. The dignity to which Mary was then raised was unparalleled and can never be paralleled. It was an occasion on which the consent of the chosen instrument of the divine counsels was most reverentially asked, and for which she had been prepared by special graces from the beginning of her existence.

Before we pass on to the visit of our Blessed Lady to St. Elizabeth, it will be well to dwell for a moment on the comparison, or rather the contrast, which the history has so often suggested to the Fathers between the first and the second Eve. In the first place, the very name given to Eve by her husband, which was not given till after the Fall, is a kind of anticipation of our Blessed Lady, as if Adam had called his wife "the mother of all living"—whereas she was in truth the mother of all doomed to die, who had introduced death into the world. This point in the comparison is brought out by St. Epiphanius and others.[1] "If you consider only external things and things obvious to sense, the origin of the whole human race on earth is derived from this same Eve. But in truth, it was from the Virgin Mary that the Life itself was introduced into the world, so that Mary should bring forth

---

1 Epiph. *Har.* 1xxviii. n. 18.

the Living One and be the Mother of the living." Whence death had come, thence life drew nigh, that in the place of death life might succeed, that He our Life Who was born of woman might shut out from us the death which had been brought in by a woman.

We shall speak presently of the contrast between the obedience of Mary and the disobedience of Eve, which forms the great feature in these comparisons of the Fathers, and which is connected so closely with the antithesis between the disobedience of Adam and the obedience of Our Lord on which St. Paul often insists.

But another point in the contrast is that which relates to the two messengers of evil and of good by whom the two virgins were addressed at the time of their trial. The one is Satan, and his object is to bring about the ruin of the whole human race by the disobedience of its first parents, and the other is Gabriel, the angel of the Incarnation, whose object is to bring about the redemption of the whole world by the obedience of Our Lord, to which the obedience of His chosen mother to the divine decree concerning herself was the necessary preliminary. Each of these angels, the evil and the good, approaches the object of his message when she is alone. But Mary is praying and Eve is idle. Satan begins by a rude and insolent question, for it called into doubt the wisdom or the goodness of God. Gabriel begins by the salutation of Our Lady in holy words which led her mind back to the prophecies and the great promises and works of God. Gabriel says "the Lord is with thee." Satan says "why hath God commanded you that you should not eat of every tree of Paradise?"

Again, the manner in which the temptation on the one hand and the salutation on the other is received is also full of contrast. Mary does not answer. She is alarmed and thinks over in her heart what manner of salutation this may be. That is, she takes refuge in her deep humility and prepares herself by thoughtful prudence for the best manner of meeting the message which God had sent her. Eve, on the other hand, answers thoughtlessly at once, without guard or precaution, as if there could be no danger in parleying with one who spoke disrespectfully of God. The very words were an invitation to disobedience, for they suggested that God should be taken to task by His creatures, that His motives, and the reasons for His commands, might be examined by those to whom these were given. Eve tells the tempter the whole of the case without reserve. He had said nothing about the tree of life as yet, but she names it as distinct from all the other trees, and she even softens the strength of the prohibition, for she says, "that we should not touch it, lest perhaps we die."

Thus she lays herself open to the temptation which was to follow; she almost courts it, she gives every handle to the cunning foe to insinuate it, to induce her to disbelieve and then to disobey God. Satan first suggests disbelief, then he lies concerning God, then he leaves the temptation to work its way with his victim by telling her that she will gain instead of losing by her disobedience. The miserable apostate suggests the very motive which had been the cause of his own fall, for he says, "you shall be as gods," and he had fallen for daring to be ambitious of rising to an equality with God.

On the other hand, St. Gabriel sets before our Blessed Lady the most magnificent acts in her favor on the part of God Himself, and he uses the prophetic words with which she was familiar in conveying his message. Eve considered only the satisfaction that she might derive from the eating of the fruit. "The woman saw that the tree was good to eat, and fair to the eyes and pleasant to behold, and she took of the fruit thereof and did eat and gave to her husband and he did eat." Mary, on the other hand, hung back from the honor out of humility, and out of her love for chastity, and when she gave her consent after the last words of St. Gabriel, it was given simply on the ground of obedience, not of the glory and dignity to which she was herself to be raised.

With Eve, the question of obedience or disobedience counted for nothing; with Mary, nothing counted but the motive of obedience. Obedience was the one virtue by which it pleased God to test His children in the Garden of Paradise. Obedience was the appointed virtue by which the world was to be redeemed by the Son of Mary. The obedience of Mary was not the cause of our redemption, but it was the forerunner of the obedience of Our Lord, and it made the Incarnation possible in the manner in which God had decreed it. The disobedience of Eve was not the cause of the ruin of the human race, because we fell in Adam, not in his wife. But the disobedience of Eve led to the disobedience of Adam, by means of which we all fell, only to be redeemed by the Son of her who said, "behold the handmaid of the Lord, be it done to me according to thy word." Eve was persuaded to doubt the word of God, daring to hope that it should not be with her and Adam according to His word. Mary believed the word of God sent to her by St. Gabriel and obeyed at once and with the most perfect faithfulness.

Thus we find these early Fathers, St. Justin Martyr, St. Irenæus and Tertullian, attributing such marvelous efficacy to the obedience of Mary. St. Justin[2] says that by the same way by which the disobedience was brought about by the serpent, by the same way it was to be put an end to. "Eve, while a virgin, and incorrupt, took in the discourse of the serpent and brought forth disobedience and death: but the Virgin Mary, who had received faith and joy, answered the Angel Gabriel, announcing to her good tidings, namely, that the Holy Ghost should come upon her and the power of the Most High overshadow her, and that therefore the Holy One to be born of her was to be the Son of God, saying,'behold the handmaid of the Lord, be it done to me according to thy word.'" St. Justin is followed by St. Irenæus his contemporary, who goes still further in attributing to the obedience of the one the reparation of the disobedience of the other. "So the knot of the disobedience of Eve receives its solution by the obedience Of Mary, for that which the virgin Eve bound by incredulity, that the Virgin Mary loosened by faith."[3] This same thought St. Irenæus repeats in the famous passage in which he says that our Blessed Lady became the advocate[4] of Eve. And there is the same doctrine contained in the passage from Tertullian usually quoted in this connection, in which he says that "Eve gave credence to the serpent, and Mary gave credence to Gabriel, and the sin committed

2 St. Justin, *Dial. a TryPh.* n. 100.

3 St. Iren. liii. 22, (33) n. 4. See also lib. v. 19.

4 Tertull. de *Cæne Christi*, c. 17.

by the credulity of Eve was blotted out by the faith of Mary." Eve was a willing, an active, a responsible agent in the work of our ruin. Mary is the same in every respect in the work of our Redemption. Neither of them was simply an involuntary unconscious instrument, whether of our Fall or of our restoration.

Chapter VII

Our Lord's Life in the Womb

One great divine reason for the immense addition of graces and spiritual gifts which we believe to have been bestowed upon our Blessed Lady immediately after the Incarnation must be found in the new position in which she was placed to Our Lord as His mother. This relation included a great variety of duties and opportunities. There is one most important element in this new position which should not be left unmentioned from the very first. The change which had taken place in the world was infinite in its intrinsic wonderfulness, and also in the duties which it imposed on the whole of creation. God had become a creature. The material universe had now in its midst its Lord and Sovereign, not as He had always been in every part of the world which He had made, but in a new mode of existence, and that a human mode. He had made Himself an Infant. He was still and could never fail to be the Lord and God of all, but He was now present among His creatures as one of them. He had thrown Himself upon them, leaving the throne and the glory and the majesty and the endless worship of heaven behind Him. He made Himself dependent on them for the homage and honor due to Him.

Mary understood what had taken place, as no one else could understand the condescension of God. She knew His worth and rights, as no one among the highest seraphs knew them. She knew what was the blessing of His presence and what the dues to His majesty. But He was her own. No ordinary presence, even as of the Blessed Sacrament in the tabernacle was that in which He dwelt in her. He had taken His Flesh and His Blood from her substance. He lived by her life. He was sustained in His human existence by her. She was nearer to Him than the priest who offers Him on the altar, nearer to him than the angels who kneel in adoration wherever He is to be found; Flesh of her flesh, Bone of her bone. She alone knew of Him. She alone was to discharge the duties of the whole visible creation in honor of Him, thanking Him, adoring Him, praising Him, loving Him for His condescension.

It will certainly help us to understand the immense grace required for a position of this kind to consider a little what that life was of Our Lord which began at the moment of the Incarnation and continued uninterruptedly for the nine months which had to pass before the first Christmas Day. It is a part of what we term in general the Holy Infancy which has a kingdom of its own in Christian devotion, like the devotion to the Babe of Bethlehem, or to the many years of the Hidden Life at Nazareth. It contains both these, for it is the Babe of Bethlehem Who is dwelling in the womb of Mary. And never was He nearly so much hidden, even in the quietest years of His life at Nazareth, as during these nine months. It is clear that each part of this great devotion has its own features and characteristics. It is also clear that this phase of it could have been practiced by no one from the beginning but our Blessed Lady herself, though at a point of time which is not directly discernible, it must have spread to St. Joseph, St. Elizabeth, St. John Baptist, St. Zachary. We shall attempt in the few following paragraphs to give a short sketch of the considerations on which this great devotion has to feed itself.

God might have become man without going through all the ordinary stages of human existence, including the first stage of all, the nine months in the womb of a mother. But He did not choose to be different from us in this respect, and the consequence of His condescension is that we have to contemplate the theological truths which are involved therein. We cannot imagine that this chain of wonderful and beautiful truths was unknown to our Blessed Lady and to St. Joseph, and to the other saints mentioned above, in the order of time in which it pleased God that it should become known. It is natural to think that the homage due to God Who had made Himself a creature was entrusted to them, and that it was not to be delayed until the humble birth at Bethlehem. A very short survey of this great field of contemplation, as we may suppose it to have been laid open to Mary and to others after her, must be enough for us here.

The history begins with the fiat of Mary. At that moment, our theology teaches us that by the action of the Holy Ghost, a part of her most pure blood was formed into the perfect Body which was to be that of Our Lord, and that at the same time, God created the human soul which was to dwell in that Body. Mary received, at the same time, a marvelous increase of grace and knowledge, corresponding, as it were, to her elevation at that moment to be the Mother of God. Here is enough for angels and saints to feed on in endless contemplation. But the knowledge of these marvels implies praise, wonder, adoration, thanksgiving, oblation, and other affections, and it is natural to suppose that these were paid duly at the time, as the knowledge concerning them was communicated to them, both by Mary and by Joseph. It is unreasonable, with the scriptural account of the Visitation before us, to exclude from this reverent worship either St. John or his parents, St. Elizabeth, and St. Zachary. But at the time of which we speak, Mary alone possessed the secret.

The next great field of contemplation under this head is that which contains the consideration of the excellencies of the sacred humanity. It became at once the highest of all God's creatures, present, past, and future. The union with the Divine Word implied the communication of all the divine perfections and the right to the adoration and homage of angels, men, and all creatures. It implied the sanctification of that soul by the substantial sanctity of God, and its being made, not only essentially holy in itself, but the source and origin of the sanctification of others. It was the Soul of the Incarnate God. It was full of all grace and the source and fountain of grace for others. It was adorned with every possible virtue in the highest perfection. And all the treasures of wisdom and knowledge thus communicated to His Soul, Our Lord directed from the first in the most perfect manner to the love and service of His Father.

The seven gifts of the Holy Ghost were in their consummate perfection in the soul of Our Lord at the first. The gift of wisdom was in Him a most lofty contemplation.

The gift of understanding showed Him all that had been arranged and decreed and foretold concerning Himself; the plan of His life and the measure of His work.

The gift of counsel showed Him exactly how every moment of His life was to be most perfectly spent and employed for the glory of the Father. The gift of fortitude secured the most ready execution of whatever the gift of counsel showed Him to be done. So it was with the other gifts. His gift of knowledge opened to His soul the full and penetrating insight into all created things. His piety filled Him with the tenderest and most just affections of reverence and love toward His Father, His Blessed Mother, St. Joseph, and all those with whom He was immediately concerned. And lastly, the gift of fear was in Him in perfection, a perfect awe and respect for the greatness of God, a deep sense of loving dependence on Him as His creature the work of His Hands.

This beautiful soul in itself, in the womb of Mary, was the object of the most tender joy and complacency and delight to God. The Eternal Father rejoiced to see His Son clothed with that human nature in which He was to do so much for the glory of His Father and for the benefit of mankind. And He rejoiced in all the treasures of grace which the sacred humanity had received for us, and for the use which His Son was to make of them in distributing them so largely and bountifully among men. It was a joy to the Eternal Son that He was now at last become Man and able to carry out the designs of His Eternal love for the Father and for us. It was a joy to the Holy Spirit to see His work accomplished and that human nature perfected by the union with the Divine Person of the Word into which He was to pour all His gifts and graces in order that they might be communicated to us.

We must next pass on to the life of Our Lord in the womb of His mother. It was a life that began at once in full vigor of mind and heart. It was a divine life, wholly directed to the glory of God, a life of merit in His sight so great as to suffice for the redemption and glorification of a thousand worlds. The soul of Jesus was perfectly conscious of, and took immense delight in, its own elevation, its union with the Divine Person, its immense gifts and privileges, its prerogative as the source of all spiritual blessings to Our Lady, St. Joseph, all the saints and all the faithful. It began at once its life of interior work for God.

The soul of Our Lord at once saw God perfectly with the plenitude of beatific vision, and here again it had this not only for Itself but also for others. To see God was to understand His infinite greatness, to adore Him with the most perfect worship as a creature, to love Him most intensely, and all creatures in Him and for Him, and especially men who had been made Our Lord's brethren by the Incarnation. Then followed gratitude, thanksgiving in His own Heart, and in the heart of His mother.

This blessed soul also saw and understood the human world into which He had come. Then came the vision of the miserable state of the race of which He was now one, its need of redemption and restoration, and the will of the Father that this should be His work. This led to His oblation of Himself for this purpose, of which St. Paul speaks in the

Epistle to the Hebrews, to His renouncement of the rights of His Body, in order that He might suffer, and the rest. The whole of His own future on earth and in heaven, as well as that of all souls, was clearly manifested to Him.

There is another head of consideration on this subject which is found in the virtues which were especially practiced by Our Lord in this life of His in the womb. He was, of course, the pattern of all virtues, but there are some which seem more particularly to belong to this period, as there are other similar circumstances in His life in the Blessed Sacrament, to which this life in the womb of Mary bears so much resemblance. Thus it may be said that Our Lord was Incarnate at the bidding of obedience, inasmuch as it was an act of obedience on the part of His mother that made the Incarnation possible and actual when it took place. Our Lady's words, "be it done to me according to thy word," were the signal for the Incarnation. He remained in the womb, for the full natural space of nine months, out of obedience. And one of His occupations in the womb was to offer Himself continually to be obedient, not only to His Eternal Father but also to all who in any way or measure represented Him, as Our Lady His mother, and St. Joseph who was to be in the place of His Father.

In the same way, when we consider the perfection of Our Lord from the moment of His conception in intelligence and the use of His faculties, we cannot but be astounded at the extreme lengths to which He went in His humiliations during this interval before His birth. The Church sings of Him, "Thou didst not abhor the Virgin's womb," and although those words may have more than one meaning, they seem to express her sense of the depths of His humiliation. It was in a manner fitting in the ways of God and to the character of Our Lord that when He had received in His human nature, the very highest possible exaltation by the union with the Divine Person of the Word, He should at once seek to humble Himself to the very utmost by His imprisonment in the womb of His mother. And yet this does not adequately express the humiliation of Our Lord, on account of His perfect consciousness and possession of all His faculties. For these enabled Him to surpass the actual humiliation of His sojourn in the womb by the affections of humiliation which His Sacred Heart conceived while there, in which He desired and decreed to humble Himself not only before God His Father and Lord but beneath the feet of the lowest and vilest of His creatures.

Another special virtue of this period of Our Lord's life is His marvelous meekness. God has become Man, but He has laid aside the majesty and the mightiness in which He appeared of old, as when He gave the Law on Mount Sinai. He is especially meek and humble of Heart, and He begins the practice of this virtue in the womb of His meek and humble mother. He begins at once to appease the anger of His Father toward men by this extreme meekness, and He prepares Himself for that exercise of it toward men in His later life which made it His most characteristic virtue. The same may be said of His practice of the love of poverty. For He is here entirely dependent on His mother for sustenance, and He has, as the Apostle says, being rich, made Himself poor for our sakes, that He might communicate to us the true riches of heaven.

Patience is another of these virtues of this stage of the infancy. This again was more to Him than to others, even this suffering of confinement and darkness and the like He increased by the interior acts of His patience. For in the womb itself, He was continually looking forward to the torments which He was to undergo, and His Heart stretched itself also to that tender sympathy which made Him make His own all the sufferings of others in the world. Such was in a special manner the exercise of prayer and contemplation, which formed the most direct occupation of the Sacred Heart during these months in which Our Lord engaged Himself in the contemplation of His Father's greatness and also in the prayerful compassion for our miseries. Such was also the practice of silence, the inseparable companion and guardian of prayer and the spirit of prayer.

In all these points, it is natural to suppose that Our Lord's Life in the womb was understood by His Blessed Mother. It was her special duty and delight to adore Him in this stage of His infinite condescension. This would be occupation enough to feed her soul and heart. All the particulars of His condition were manifested to His mother.

It was Mary's office to honor Him in the name of all, to sympathize with His humiliation and His sufferings, to join her heart with His in the continual stream of loving acts of thankfulness and adoration and self-oblation which rose from Him before the throne of His Father. We cannot doubt that the presence of Our Lord with her in this most marvelous way was a grace which raised her daily higher and higher in her most consummate perfection. We are nowhere told of the secret intercourse and converse, which united the hearts of Jesus and Mary in a continual exchange of the most fervent affections at this time. This is a secret of heaven, though we cannot doubt that every movement and thought of our Blessed Lady must have been divinely influenced thereby. No heart was like hers for perfect docility to interior movements and the inspirations of God. Her position with regard to our Blessed Lord was altogether unique, in heaven and on earth.

If Our Lord can be so lavish of His interior converse, as we see Him to have been in the case of some of the saints especially at times such as that of Holy Communion, it is only rational to think that the communication of His secrets and other messages, Heart to heart, with His Blessed Mother, must have been far surpassing anything of which record remains to us. We can understand how sublime and interior a life she must now have led until the time when Our Lord came forth from her sacred womb in the stable of Bethlehem.

Chapter VIII

The Visitation

St. Luke i. 39–56. Vita Vitæ Nostræ, § 5.

There can be little doubt that the Annunciation and the Incarnation were immediately followed by the Visitation, as we call it, of our Blessed Lady. The manner in which this mystery is related by St. Luke, who seems to speak of Our Lady as if she were altogether alone in her journey, suggests the opportunity of some remarks on the relation of these Gospel narratives to the actual history which it is well to make at the outset of the part of our work on which we are now engaged. It is well also to remind ourselves of certain truths concerning the manner of the dealings of God with souls, as well as concerning the formation of the Gospel history as we have to form it, which may help us the better to understand the narrative on which we shall now for some time be occupied.

It appears to have been the plan of God that St. Joseph, whatever he might think or surmise, or even know, in a human and ordinary way concerning the mystery which had taken place, was to be left without any divine direction concerning it until the time came when his own action was requisite for the carrying on of the sacred mystery. In this, God only proceeded in the way which He so often follows, of leaving His saints in the dark about His future decrees concerning themselves until the necessary moment comes. For the delay which is thus secured for the silent working of His graces in the hearts which are so dear to Him is often the most precious opportunity which is afforded them in a whole life for the exercise of the most sublime virtues. It may be a period of exquisite trial, but a trial exquisitely corresponded to by a patience, a humility, a charity, a prudence, and an exercise of confidence in God under difficulties which may win for the person who is thus tried the very highest of crowns.

It was characteristic of Eve that she should go at once to Adam with her miserable discovery of the sweetness of the forbidden fruit. Mary kept her secret to herself and to her God, leaving it to Him to reveal it in His own time and way to St. Joseph, confident that the time and the way which He would choose would be the best for her and the best for her spouse. She might hope, but she could not know, what was to be the counsel of God as to her husband's future position to her or her Child. But in so mighty and lofty a mystery, every detail was in the hand of God alone. On the other hand, God was to give to St. Joseph the opportunity of that peculiar and unique trial to which his faithfulness was exposed and which we shall have presently to endeavor to explain.

Let us now apply these truths to the narrative before us of the Visitation. It is entirely confined to the briefest possible account of the doings of our Blessed Lady. "And Mary rising up in those days, went into the hill country in haste, into a city of Juda, and she entered into the house of Zachary, and saluted Elizabeth." Such is this simple statement, and if we were to suppose that it tells us all that passed, we might imagine that Our Lady, a young and most modest bride, left her home without any communication with her husband, and travelled a distance of two or three days' journey at least, alone and unguarded. If this had been the case, it is probable we should have been told how it was that so extraordinary a course was taken by her without any direct guidance from God. It is impossible to suppose, in the first place, that she took this journey without the cognizance and permission of St. Joseph. He had over her movements the rights of a husband, and she is not likely to have been guided to disregard them.

In the second place, there is no reason at all for supposing that she took this journey unaccompanied by St. Joseph. The Annunciation took place at the time of the year when it was the custom of the Jews to resort to Jerusalem for the great feast of the Pasch. We know from St. Luke that it was, a few years later than this, the custom of St. Joseph and our Blessed Lady to go up from Nazareth at this time. It is most likely that this devotion had been practiced by them from the very beginning. Thus the opportunity for the journey of Mary may well have been furnished by the incidence of the great feast almost immediately after the Annunciation. She might go to Judæa with her husband and on the way to the feast. The town in which St. Zachary and St. Elizabeth lived was some distance beyond Jerusalem, and thus it seems certain that St. Joseph would accompany Our Lady, after they had paid their devotions in the Holy City, to the home of her kinswoman.

She was the mother of the unborn King, but she would make herself humble in all things, and her motive in this journey may have been principally one of charity, hoping that, as St. Elizabeth was old and infirm, she might be of use in waiting upon her. Nor could she find any occupation more congenial to her own humility than thus to make herself the handmaid of the mother of the Precursor. She at once lowers herself where she can and makes herself the servant of Elizabeth.

But though this had been the chief motive of Mary in her journey, God had other and higher aims in bringing it about. For it was His design to use her presence, and that of Our Lord in her womb, for the sanctification of St. John in the womb of his mother, and for the filling St. Elizabeth herself with the Holy Ghost and the spirit of prophecy. These great blessings were to be conferred through the presence of Our Lady at once, and as she was to remain for nearly three months in the house of her cousin, it must be supposed that the benefit of her abiding presence and continual conversation was not less great than that of her first salutation.

The salutation of our Blessed Lady to her cousin was probably the ordinary greeting of love and affection. But the words of Mary, who had within her womb the Incarnate God, were words of power as well as simply the goodwill of the speaker. Thus, the moment that they sounded in the ears of St. Elizabeth, two wonderful outpourings of grace followed. One of them affected the infant Baptist in his mother's womb, while the other wrought wonderful effects in his mother herself. St. Elizabeth was the first to hear the blessed words of the salutation of Mary, but the effect of grace appears to have followed first in her infant son. The words struck on the ears of the mother, but their power first reached the soul of St. John. Their effect was his sanctification in the womb, that gift which had been predicted for him by St. Gabriel when he was commissioned to announce to his father Zachary the conception of the Precursor. Gabriel had said that he was to be filled with the Holy Ghost even from his mother's womb. Up to that moment, the soul and body of the Baptist had shared the common lot of the souls and bodies of all infants born of the race of Adam. They lay under the ban of original sin. The prayers of his holy parents had risen continually for St. John, ever since his conception.

The voice of our Blessed Lady, which conveyed the power of the divine Infant Who lived in her womb, altered the whole state of the blessed child of Elizabeth. The whole existence of the child, dark and sad and sombre, was full of light and joy and life. The chains fell off, the bonds of original sin, the imperfections and penalties of the state of estrangement from his Creator. He was at once awakened by divine grace to the full use of his faculties, and the streams of grace, bearing on their bosom the virtues—theological, moral, and infused—and the gifts of the Holy Ghost, poured themselves into and over his soul. He broke out at once into the full exercise of faith and hope and charity. He knew the presence of Our Lord. The change which in others is gradual and progressive was made in him in a moment.

The sun rose on him in a moment, without any preceding twilight. And at the presence of his Lord and Savior, he, the first of all except the Blessed Mother, manifested by outward sign his joy and love and reverence and homage. He leapt in the womb for joy.

At the same time, another great operation of grace was going on in the soul of the blessed Elizabeth herself. It is commonly said by the Fathers who have spoken on this mystery, that the Child was first illuminated and then the mother, and that the divine illumination passed from the soul of the Child to the soul of the mother. Elizabeth was filled with the Holy Ghost. She received the full illumination needed for her comprehension of the mystery. She may have known something of her wonderful gifts from her birth. She may have been present at her presentation in the Temple. She may have marveled what was to be the destiny of one so singularly marked out for great things by the circumstances of her birth and childhood. But she could have had no thought of the dignity to which she had now been raised. But as soon as the voice of her salutation sounded in her ears, the infant leaped in her womb for joy.

These simple words contain the whole of what we have been saying about the sanctification of the Baptist, and they also signify the cause of the further grace now bestowed on his mother. Elizabeth understood by a divine light, what had taken place. She understood the mystery of the Incarnation, the fulfillment of the prophecies, the beginning of the accomplishment of the salvation of the world. She knew that Our Lord was there present in the womb of His mother. She understood the leaping of her babe in her own womb as his greeting and joyous homage to the Incarnate King, and that it was no simply natural or involuntary movement, but the deliberate expression of joy.

"Elisabeth was filled with the Holy Ghost and she cried out with a loud voice and said, 'Blessed art thou among women, and blessed is the fruit of thy womb! And whence is this to me, that the mother of my Lord should come to me? For behold, as soon as the voice of thy salutation sounded in my ears, the infant in my womb leaped for joy. And blessed art thou that hast believed, because those things shall be accomplished that were spoken to thee by the Lord.'"

St. Elizabeth spoke under the immediate impulse of the Holy Ghost, moved so strongly that she cannot contain herself. "Blessed art thou among women!" These words are the last words of Gabriel's salutation and the first of hers. She adds the other words, "blessed is the fruit of thy womb," showing that she knew of the accomplishment of the mystery. Both Mary and the fruit of her womb are blessed in the highest degree and measure. But He is the source of all blessing; He cannot be otherwise than most blessed, because He is the Incarnate God. Mary, in all her blessedness, receives from His fullness in this as in all other respects. The next words of St. Elizabeth seem the natural acknowledgment and honor done to her by the visit of her cousin. "Whence is this to me?" What merit is there in me, that, when I ought to be waiting on her and paying my homage to her, the Mother of my Lord should instead come to me? Then she goes on to declare the wonderful effect, in herself and in her Child, which have followed from the salutation of Mary.

The reason and cause of the knowledge of St. Elizabeth concerning the Incarnation was that she was filled with the

Holy Ghost, and especially for the purpose of her being a witness to, and a companion of, Mary. The leaping of her Child in the womb was evidence to her of the change that had been wrought in him by the presence of the unborn God and the voice of His Blessed Mother. She knew that the fruit of the womb of Mary was most blessed because He was at that moment manifesting His spiritual power, as present in Mary, by the sanctification of His Precursor. Thus the exultation of the Child in her womb was evidence of the presence of the Incarnate God in the womb of Mary, and not only of His presence, but of the active exercise by Him of that power of sanctification which belonged to Him alone.

He came to be the prophet of the Highest, and now he anticipated his office and declared preternaturally the presence of his Lord. St. Elizabeth goes on at once to speak of the blessedness of Mary. She is not only the blessed among women, as having been chosen from all eternity to be the Mother of God, but also as having corresponded most faithfully and most perfectly in the time of her trial to the designs of God. This is the meaning of the last clause of the greeting of St. Elizabeth, "Blessed thou that didst believe, because those things shall be accomplished that were spoken to thee by the Lord." This shows us that St. Elizabeth was divinely enlightened as to what had passed between the angel and our Blessed Lady, and that she now is commissioned to give a further assurance to her that the great promises shall be accomplished.

This prophecy of St. Elizabeth shows us the very close connection between the two mysteries of the Incarnation and Visitation. It may be said that the former mystery is incomplete without the latter. Not that anything could be added to the truth and completeness of the Incarnation by any number of subsequent mysteries, but that the divine counsels required that the relation between these two mysteries should be established through the confirmation of the former by the circumstances of the latter. We have seen that the last words of St. Gabriel at the Annunciation referred to the conception of the Precursor in the womb of St. Elizabeth, and they implied that it was the will of God that Mary should immediately undertake the journey which ended in the Visitation.

It is easy to see how much is added to the splendor of the Incarnation by the Visitation. The Visitation gave God the opportunity of declaring, by a series of marvels of the highest kind, that what He had promised to Mary by the mouth of Gabriel had already been performed as far as the Incarnation of His Son and that it would be still further carried out, in due time, by the exaltation of the Child of Mary. And the close connection between the two mysteries may be further seen in the fact that it is not till the Visitation is completed that Our Lady breaks forth into her great canticle of thanksgiving, of which we shall begin to speak in the following chapter.

Chapter IX

The Canticle of Mary

St. Luke i. 46–56. Vita Vitæ Nostræ, § 5.

Up to this time, the Blessed Virgin had said nothing about herself, or the great blessing which had been bestowed on her. The Holy Ghost inspired the exultation of the infant in the womb of her cousin and the exclamation of St. Elizabeth. Thus it was now necessary for her to speak, that she might turn the praise away from herself to Him to Whom all praise, all glory, all gratitude, are due; the simple fact that she now speaks, and for the purpose and to the effect for which she speaks, is a fresh revelation to us of the character of Mary.

But the canticle of which we are now to speak is not only important to us as the revelation of the thoughts of our Blessed Lady herself. For the thoughts of Mary are the thoughts suggested to her by her Divine Son. Thus they breathe to us the first inspirations of His Sacred Heart, as well as the affections of His Blessed Mother. The Canticle of Mary stands first among the canticles of the New Testament. It gives them their character and dominant note. Mary is now speaking in her own person, but more than this, she speaks as the representative of the Church, of the whole human race redeemed by the great mercy of the Incarnation. She is uttering the first hymn of thanksgiving of the whole creation which has been renovated and elevated by that mighty mystery. Her *Magnificat* sounds on and on in all ages of the Church, the accompaniment, to the great sacrifice of thanksgiving which is perpetually offered all over the world in the Blessed Eucharist. The meaning of these few and simple words can never be so fathomed as to exhaust it. There is no thanksgiving, and loving gratitude, which cannot find here its fitting expression, just as no petition, or prayer, can find itself adequately expressed in the prayer taught us by Our Lord. All prayers are summed up in the Lord's Prayer, and all thanksgivings are summed up in the *Magnificat*.

The *Magnificat* begins by the note of thanksgiving. This is in some measure suggested by the praises of St. Elizabeth. But it is also the natural and peculiar note of the New Testament. The whole of the Old Testament was a looking forward with desire to the blessing of which Mary was now the living and conscious instrument and home. The promises on which the saints of the Old Testament lived were now fulfilled in her. The whole of the Old Testament had been the intense longing of the world for its deliverer. The New Testament has another duty to fulfill, that of thanking God for the accomplishment of His promises. Thus the characteristic of the New Testament is joyous thanksgiving, and the first word of this affection to God is spoken by the Mother of God in the house of St. Elizabeth. We see the spirit of the *Magnificat* all through the New Testament. It meets us over and over again in the Epistles of St. Paul. If thankfulness and rejoicing are the characteristic graces of the Christian Church, every note of hers in which they are breathed is an echo of the *Magnificat* of Mary.

Mary is thus our first Christian teacher, as well as the mother of our God in His human nature. For the nine months between the Incarnation and the Nativity, she was His one great worshipper. And now that she has to speak and to leave behind her a record, in which the affections of her heart are enshrined for our use, we may well take her utterances as given to us by God as our lesson in this respect. The subject of her song is Our Lord, the Incarnate God. She speaks of herself only in reference to Him and her position with Him, which involves our own relations to herself. One thing more must be added by way of preface. Our Blessed Lady takes as her pattern, and as the foundation of her canticle, one of the canticles of the Old Testament, the canticle of Anna the mother of Samuel, a song of thanksgiving which we cannot doubt had been taught her by her own mother, St. Anne. She uses also language taken from other parts of Sacred Scripture. Her mind ranges over the whole of the dealings of God with man in the way of mercy, and over the whole of the records of those dealings as contained in the inspired books. It is impossible to doubt that the sequence of thought in the *Magnificat* is to a large extent in direct correspondence with the sequence of thought in the canticle of Anna.

We shall find that the canticle of Our Lady takes us back in thought to the scene in paradise when the first great promise was made to man. It is the song of thanksgiving of the second Eve for the immense privileges bestowed upon her, and it is also her song of triumph over the enemies allotted to her by the decree of God Himself in the first promise and prophecy. We may now go on to the first strophe of the *Magnificat*.

"And Mary said, My soul doth magnify the Lord, and my spirit hath rejoiced in God my Savior, because He hath regarded the humility of His handmaiden, for behold, from henceforth, all generations shall call me Blessed." There may be in these first words something of an answer to the lofty praises which had been uttered concerning her by cousin St. Elizabeth, but the answer is couched in the words of Scripture, and rises beyond the immediate occasion. This is Mary's version of the beginning of the canticle of Anna, "My heart hath rejoiced in the Lord and my horn is exalted in my God." Her rejoicing in her Jesus is something founded on her magnifying of her God, and at the same time something greater, in that it is more to have God as her Savior than to have Him simply as her Lord. In the subjection to God all creation shares, in the salvation wrought by Our Lord not all creatures share. The second blessing is the extension of the first, the second affection is the fruit of the first, and yet something more than the first.

When it is said by Our Lady that her soul magnifies the Lord, it may be meant that her whole being is occupied in praising, glorifying, honoring, and adoring God. And when it is said that her spirit rejoices in God her Savior, it appears to be meant that all the higher faculties of the intelligent being which God has given her are flooded with the light and intense joy which naturally belong to the loftiest contemplations of which a created intelligence is capable.

For her whole mind and heart and being are engaged in magnifying God, in giving Him all the homage and worship and thanks which His infinite goodness and greatness deserve at her hands, while her spiritual faculties especially are filled with the highest of all affections.

The words of Our Lady set before us an immense range of benefits which she has received from God. When she speaks in the first clause of magnifying the Lord, we may consider that she is dwelling in thought on the great displays of God's goodness to her in all that is embraced by His dealings with her as her God. And when she speaks in the second clause of rejoicing in God her Jesus, we may consider that she has before her mind and heart, as the object of thanksgiving and the most intense joy, all that God has done for her in the order of redemption. We all receive from Him this twofold treasure of blessings and gifts, what He gives us as our Creator, our Father, our Provider, in the first place, and what He gives to us in the second place, as our Incarnate Savior, the Redeemer of our souls and bodies.

We may consider that the words of which we are speaking show us that our Blessed Lady habitually fed her thoughts and contemplations on the greatness and goodness of God and that she constantly raised her heart in thanksgiving. No one but herself could count out so faithfully the immense series of those wonderful benefits. The long list of blessings began in that eternal love of God for her which had no beginning and was to have no end, and which was the original fountain, the perennial source, of all the gifts bestowed upon her, whether in the order of nature or in the order of grace. It was from this love that had proceeded her election and predestination to the position she was to occupy in the kingdom of her Son. It had poured itself out in the creation of her most perfect body and soul, in the grace of her immaculate conception, and in the immense dowry of gifts which accompanied that unique privilege.

We do not often attempt to give to ourselves an account of the wonderful gifts which we have received from God and the gratitude of Mary may be an example and an incentive to us of careful and particular thanksgiving.

"My soul doth magnify the Lord!" To magnify the Lord is to form the highest and largest conceptions of His greatness and goodness, to form those conceptions into the shape of mental and most heartfelt praise and estimation, and then to pour this praise out in whatever way is open to the heart or soul in which they spring up.

We cannot really magnify God. That is, we cannot make Him greater than He is, but we can most truly enlarge and deepen our conceptions concerning Him; we can extend our appreciation and knowledge of Him by the consideration of His works. For all increase of our appreciation of Him is an increase of our power of praising Him for what we more and more appreciate. This is in truth the occupation of the angels in heaven, who are ever learning more and more to understand God, and this will be the blissful occupation of the saints and blessed in heaven throughout all eternity. Our Lady's words include all that is here suggested. They show us her characteristic grace of contemplation and study of the divine attributes and works. They illustrate what is said of her, more than once, in this part of the Gospel of St. Luke, that she kept all that passed and pondered it in her heart, as the mysteries of the Incarnation were, one after another, unfolded before her and in her. The hymn which the Church has caught from the angels, the *Gloria in excelsis*, is but an expansion of the first words of the *Magnificat*. It contains the glorification of God, not simply for His works as Creator, but especially for His work as Redeemer. The words open to us the heart of the Blessed Mother, the first of pure creatures, and they reveal to us also the affections of the Sacred Heart itself, then beating and glowing with love in the womb of Mary. Thus it is the song of the Church, for where can her children learn a more perfect expression of the affections which they ought to conceive toward God than from the hearts of Jesus and Mary?

But we must pass on to the second clause of this opening strophe of this great canticle.

It refers to that second great ocean of graces and gifts poured into her soul, as the fruit of the Redemption wrought for her by her Son, as well as for all the rest of the world.

Others were redeemed after they had been touched by sin. She was redeemed that she might not be touched by sin. In others, sin is pardoned and atoned for; in her, it was shut out by a plenitude of graces paid for by the passion of her Son. Most truly, therefore, is He to her a Jesus, more than to all others, by the ransom He has paid for her, the share He has given her of His merits, the dignity to which He has raised her, and the glory which corresponds to that dignity and to the love with which He regards her.

The holy affection of joy of which Our Lady here speaks, is the very highest and most tender of all spiritual affections. Joy is the very life of God Himself. Thus when Our Lord speaks of the very highest consummation of the blessedness which awaits the saints in heaven as their reward, He says that it will be said to them, "Enter into the joy of thy Lord." When then our Blessed Lady speaks of her spirit rejoicing in God her Savior, she speaks of something even beyond the contemplation and magnification of God, of His greatness. She speaks of the enjoyment of His sweetness and ineffable beauty as her own. Joy is the crown and flower and essence of the life of the holy angels in heaven; it is imparted in a measure to the saints and servants of God even upon earth, and of course, it was imparted in a pre-eminent and singular measure to the one heart which was the heart of the chosen mother.

Our Blessed Lady changes the words of the prophet for he had said that he would rejoice, and she says that her spirit has rejoiced. He was looking forward in hope to the promised Incarnation of the Son of God. But Mary has already received Our Lord, the hope of the prophets came into her sacred womb, and that moment of ineffable bliss and delight remains with her forever, not as a memory but as a joy ever fresh, because it is ever renewed and intensified. She can never be other than the Mother of God, and she can never lose the joy of becoming the Mother of God. This great treasure of holiest affections Our Lady sums up in the few words in which she declares that her spirit hath rejoiced in God her Savior.

The second part of this first strophe of the canticle passes to another head of the benefits of God to Mary. For what she has hitherto spoken of are benefits which are in their measure common to her with all mankind. We do not all receive in equal abundance these great gifts the blessings of creation and providence and preservation.

In any case, everyone has a share of the common blessings which God lavishes upon all, but besides thee, everyone also has a long list of personal and particular favors for which to magnify God and for which to rejoice in God his Savior. Thus, our Blessed Lady, after having glorified God for the blessings which are common to her with all, goes on to commemorate the particular favors for which she is debtor to His exceeding peculiar and personal love.

Our Lady's words are that she magnifies the Lord and rejoices in God her Savior, "because He hath regarded the humility of His handmaiden, for behold from henceforth all generations shall call me blessed." It is probable that the words are cast in the form by way of an antithesis between the qualities which our Blessed Lady has been contemplating in her God and those which she finds in herself. The greatness of God which she magnifies is contrasted with the littleness, the nothingness, of one who is nothing more than His servant. The title of Lord answers to the title of handmaiden, and the greatness of God answers to the humility which Our Lady sees in herself.

He has regarded the low estate of His handmaiden with favor and exceeding mercy and love, raising her to the very highest position that can be occupied by a creature.

"For behold from henceforth all generations shall call me blessed." St. Elizabeth had called Our Lady blessed among women on the score of her great faith. But the blessing itself which was granted to her was something most lofty and unique in itself, and it is this that Our Lady seems to imply when she says, "Behold from henceforth all generations shall call me blessed." The blessing lay in the incommunicable gift of being made the Mother of the Incarnate Word. It is this, therefore, and not the faith which her cousin had spoken of, that is the cause why all generations shall call her blessed. All her privileges and gifts are based on this one great act of divine condescension. For the Incarnation is a work of God which can never pass away or be undone, and therefore the blessing which it brings with it to the chosen mother can never pass away or change.

The act of God in making her His mother is the fertile source of all the blessings which she is to inherit, a spring of life, forever welling up in fresh glories and honors, as its fruits manifest themselves and multiply themselves more and more generation after generation. As the fruitfulness of the Incarnation is ever fresh and ever increasing in its applications and manifestations, so in the same way does the glory and blessedness of Mary increase and spread itself more and more widely, and higher and higher, with that fruitfulness of the Incarnation in which she has borne her part and in which she has a share. She can never be other than the Mother of God, and every effect of the Incarnation is an effect of her consent, in the great work of God.

For it is not possible to think rightly and adequately of the Incarnation without recognizing the elevation of the Mother of God. All heresies against the Person of Our Lord contain the denial of her blessedness, and as the Church sings of her, she has destroyed all heresies in all the world, because the true doctrine concerning her refutes all of them. All the faithful, everywhere and at all times, re-echo the words of the woman who lifted up her voice out of the crowd to Our Lord, saying, "Blessed the womb that bare Thee and the breasts which gave Thee suck." These words contain the whole Christian theology concerning her.

Our Lady's words thus imply the foreknowledge of all this glory, as if she had before the eyes of her mind the whole of that immense honor which was to show itself in the countless devotions of the whole Church all over the world for her glorification. She sees the endless glory on earth and in heaven which was to be hers, and she humbly lays it all at the feet of God from Whom it comes. All was to be His gift, and all was to be given back to Him.

The dwellers in heaven and on earth and in purgatory, all and everywhere and at every time, in every stage of the world's history, all who acknowledge Our Lord as their Redeemer are to acknowledge also the singular beatitude and grace of her who is made His mother.

We may now pass on to what we may call the second strophe or part in this great canticle. Our Lady speaks of God as having manifested Himself mainly in the exercise of three of His great attributes in His dealing with herself. These three attributes are His power, His holiness, and His mercy. "Because He that is mighty hath done great things to me, and His name is Holy, and His mercy is from generation unto generation to them that fear Him." For the Incarnation is at once the greatest possible exertion of the power of God, the greatest possible manifestation of His holiness, and also the greatest possible exertion of His divine mercy.

The thoughts here suggested are inexhaustible in their range and extent, but a few words must suffice to sketch out the immense field thus opened out to us. The whole of the great act of power which was required for the Incarnation is contained in the gift of Himself to Mary as His mother, and therefore He that is mighty hath done great things to her.

In the second place, our Blessed Lady speaks of the Holiness of God as manifested in His dealings with her. The Incarnation was, in the first place, the one special work of the holiness of God, in the work which it accomplished, and in the fruits it has produced on earth and in heaven. But especially we may suppose that our Blessed Lady means to pour out her heart in thanksgiving for the personal graces bestowed upon herself as the chosen instrument of this most divine work. She knew, in the language of St. Paul, the gifts that had been given her by God, and she raised her voice in thankfulness for them.

And, in the third place, Our Lady celebrates the mercy of God. The Incarnation was a work of infinite power, and a work of infinite holiness. But the power and the holiness were, so to say, the means for the accomplishment of a great design of mercy. Mercy, indeed the Incarnation, would have been in itself, as the Creation of the world was, an act of mercy, even if there had been no fallen race to be redeemed, no debt of infinite justice to be paid thereby. But in truth, it was a work of mercy, of restoration, and reconciliation, and atonement, and satisfaction, besides being a work of infinite condescension and compassion, such as might have been manifested by the elevation of a created race to union with its Lord and Creator, though the created race had never offended His justice, or made itself liable to His wrath.

We must fully understand the unworthiness of the offenders and their entire dependence on Him, the ingratitude, the full light with which they sinned, the utter impossibility of any due compensation on their part to the justice which they had outraged, the hopelessness of any fitting reconciliation by any efforts on their own part. And then must be added the magnificence of the atoning sacrifice, the dignity of the Victim, the plenteousness of the redemption wrought out by Him, the immense height to which the fallen race were to be raised, and the depth of the humiliation by which this was to be bought. In all these respects, there is no work of God in which He has so wonderfully manifested His mercy as in the Incarnation.

Our Blessed Lady speaks, moreover, of the mercy of God which is from generation unto generations on them that fear Him. In this, she seems to refer to the special characteristic of the divine counsel of mercy which was now finally accomplished in the Incarnation. That the fruits of the Incarnation were always available from the beginning of the world, even though the actual atonement for sin and the reconciliation of man with God were not brought about till the fullness of time, as the Apostle speaks. Our Lord, as St. John calls Him in the Apocalypse, was the Lamb slain from the foundation of the world. Thus from the very first the fruit of the Precious Blood which was to be shed on Calvary could be applied to the souls of all those who did their part to secure the effects of that great future sacrifice. Thus our Blessed Lady's words carry us back to the first promise made before the expulsion of the fallen pair from paradise, and she brings out, as a special cause for her thanksgiving, this most tender and careful provision of God Who, while He determined not to grant the favor of the Incarnation immediately on the Fall, still provided that its benefits should not be delayed and held back until the full debt had been paid to His justice, according to His decree.

Her heart and mind seem to stretch themselves to the whole breadth and length of God's mercifulness so as to leave no part of it unacknowledged and uncelebrated.

Such are some of the truths contained in this part of the *Magnificat*. Our Lady lifts up her voice to commemorate and make known the exercise in the Incarnation of these three great attributes of which we have been speaking—the power, the holiness, and the mercy of God. She does this in her own name, and in the name of the Church and the whole race of Adam. She is herself the greatest instance of the working of God's power; she has received more than all others together of the communication of His holiness, and she is herself the greatest object of His compassionate mercy. She has received far more than all, as her elevation is so far above that of all others, and she is made also, by a special provision of His love, the vessel of mercy, in the sense that she not only receives grace for herself but has also the privilege of being the channel of graces to others, not as we all receive of the fullness of grace which is in Our Lord, but because it is her special office to have a part in the shedding on all others by the patronage and intercession which belong to her as the mother of the Redeemer, the streams of His grace.

Holy Anna speaks in general of the wonderful way in which God shows His care for His people and for His anointed. Zachary speaks of the God of Israel visiting and working the redemption of His people. But he is not himself the channel or the instrument of these mercies. But in the words of Mary, there is something more. She is, as it were, taken up into the counsels of God; she is made the depository of the treasures of the graces of the Incarnation. The great work is wrought in her in the first instance, and because of this, it is that all generations are to call her blessed.

Having thus celebrated the great attributes of God as manifested in the mystery carried out in her sacred womb, our Blessed Lady proceeds to describe, in the words of Sacred Scripture, the particulars of the great work of mercy and power which has been wrought.

Our Blessed Lady's words: "He hath showed might in His arm, He hath scattered the proud in the conceit of their hearts. He hath put down the mighty from their seat and hath exalted the humble. He hath filled the hungry with good things, and the rich He hath sent empty away." We have now to consider the meaning of these words in the mouth of Our Lady, and to see what precisely is the action of God which she thus celebrates.

The words are used by Our Lord in His account of the Publican and the Pharisee, as conveying a general principle. God alone is great, God alone has any true excellence or beauty of His own, and He will not bear that the poor worms of earth should dare to take to themselves as their own any glory or honor which does not belong to them. For to do this is to lie. It is in a manner incumbent on God in His providence to put down the proud. He loves humility because it is truth, because it gives all glory to Him. And we know that some of the saints have said that it was the love of humility that drew Him down from heaven to become Man. It has a beauty to Him which He cannot, as it were, resist.

But we must suppose that these words of our Blessed Lady refer, particularly and especially, to some one great or greatest instance of this wonderful law of the dealings of God with His creatures.

What then, we must ask, was the particular exertion of the power of God of which she speaks, when she says, "He hath showed might in His arm"? Of whom in particular was she thinking when she rejoiced because He hath scattered the proud in the conceit of their hearts? Who are the mighty ones whom she means when she says that "He hath put down the mighty from their seat," and who are those whom He has raised on high when she gives thanks because "He hath exalted the humble"? And in the same way, who are "the hungry who are filled with good things," and who are "the rich who are sent away empty"?

The subject of the whole of this canticle is the great power and goodness of God as displayed in the Incarnation, and this being laid down as a general principle, we must find the special meaning of these words in something which was brought about in and by the Incarnation. The Incarnation itself is the great work of might which Our Lady says God hath showed in His arm. The arm of God is the scriptural expression for His power or might, but it seems to be sometimes used distinctly for the Incarnate Son, Who as St. Paul says "is the power of God."[1] It is in that mystery that we must find the explanation of the words of Our Lady. The expression of scattering the proud is taken from one of the great historical psalms, where we find the words, "Thou hast humbled the proud one as one that is slain, with the arm of Thy strength Thou hast scattered Thy enemies."[2]

This leads us to this conclusion: the proud who are scattered in the conceit of their hearts must be these proud beings who have been humbled and defeated and brought to naught by the incarnation of the Son of God. The mighty who are put down from their seat are those whose empire and principality have been annihilated by the Incarnation. The humble who are exalted and set on high are those who have been so exalted by the Incarnation. Thus it seems plain that Our Lady's words refer primarily to the rebel angels, who have been scattered in more than one way in the conceit of their hearts. We are told by some of the Fathers that Satan and his associates turned away in scorn from the idea of worshipping their God in the inferior nature of a man which He was to take upon Him. They thought themselves worthy, and able and strong enough, to seize the highest thrones in heaven, to make themselves equal with God. They thought they would owe allegiance and obedience to no one. And this very thought of their hearts was like a poison working in their whole being, taking from them all true power and strength, all wisdom and happiness, turning them into

1 I Cor. i. 24.

2 Psalm 1xxxviii. 11.

devils, much as if the lifeblood of a man had been turned into fire, and remained forever to course through his veins as the cause of unutterable torment.

This was the conceit of their heart, to turn away from God in their pride and rebellion. And the thought itself separated them forever from the one object of their love, the one cause of their happiness. And having been cast down from the most glorious and happy condition which was anywhere to be found among the creatures of God, they became at once the most miserable and the most hopeless. This was the first scattering of the proud in the conceit of their hearts in the history of creation. And then by virtue of the humiliation of the Son of God to an inferior nature, which had been their great stumbling block, the race of man was raised in their place to the inheritance of the thrones in heaven which they had forfeited so that God might be forever glorified, not only in the casting down of the proud but also in the exaltation of the humble in their place, which are wrought by the Incarnation.

Again, the rebel angels conceived the thought of dragging down to the misery of their own fall the race of Adam. They tempted our first parents, envious of their innocent happiness, and also hating them with a special hatred because they were destined to succeed to those blessed homes with God which they had themselves been once intended to fill. And so in the conceit of their hearts, they devised, and even brought about, the fall of man. And then once more, the conceit of their own hearts became the cause of their more utter ruin and humiliation. His enemies might seem to triumph, but their triumph was to be turned to their own destruction. They had counted on the justice of God. They made no account of His mercy. They could not penetrate the secrets of His wisdom. The most enlightened intelligences in heaven, of the Cherubim and Seraphim, could not have devised what God was about to do. No one but God could have thought of it and no one but God could have executed it. God Himself became man and satisfied His own justice by becoming man. He raised the fallen race, not only to the height which it might have attained if it had never fallen, but far higher. This was to be the effect of the humiliation of Jesus Christ, Whom Our Lady carried in her womb when she sang this song of triumph. The elevation of man corresponded to the humiliation of the Son of God, and what Our Lady has in her mind is that wonderful exaltation founded on that still more wonderful humiliation. Here again, the Incarnation is the cause of all.

The commentary on these words of the *Magnificat* might perhaps be found in two pregnant passages of St. Paul. In the first, he speaks of the humiliation of Our Lord, both in the Incarnation and in the Passion. "Let this mind be in you which was also in Christ Jesus, Who being in the form of God thought it not robbery to be equal with God, but emptied Himself, taking the form of a servant, being made in the likeness of man and in habit found as a man. He humbled Himself, becoming obedient unto death, even to the death of the cross. For which cause God also hath highly exalted Him, and hath given Him a name which is above all names, that at the name of Jesus every knee should bow, of those that are in heaven, on earth, and under the earth, and that every tongue should confess that the Lord Jesus is in the glory of God the Father."[3] Here we have the last portion of the passage of the *Magnificat*, the exaltation of the humble, whether on earth or in heaven, in time or in eternity. For in the exaltation of Our Lord, as the reward of His humiliation, the whole principle and cause of the exaltation of all who follow Him in His humility are contained.

In the other great passage, to the Colossians, the Apostle draws out the other part of the words of the Mother of God, those which relate to the scattering of the proud. He speaks of Our Lord as "blotting out the handwriting of the decree that was against us, which was contrary to us," the decree of the justice of God which was brought upon us by the sin which the evil angel suggested to our first parents. "And He hath taken it out of the way fastening it to the cross, and spoiling the principalities and powers, He hath exposed them confidently in open show, triumphing over them in Himself."[4]

These two passages taken together may be considered as giving a complete picture of this great work of God, of which Our Lady here speaks. The might God hath showed in His arm is the benefit of the Incarnation. The proud are the evil angels whom St. Paul speaks of as the principalities and powers, who were so proud as to seek to be equal with God, and to these St. Paul alludes in his words about Our Lord not "thinking it robbery" to be equal with God. The conceit of their hearts, in which they have been scattered, is the evil design and counsel which they had conceived, and which in every case, and in all particulars, turned out to

---

3 Philip. ii. 5–11.

4 Col. ii. 14, 15.

their greater confusion. For their design to rise to the highest throne of heaven led to their being cast down into hell. Their plot to seduce man in which they seemed to succeed led to the overwhelming mercy of the Incarnation and the redemption thereby.

The great crime of the Passion was brought about by them, and it seemed to their malicious hearts the greatest of their triumphs. Here again they were scattered in the conceit of their hearts. For by the Passion, they brought about their own entire overthrow, and if they had desired to contribute to the glory of God, to the honor of Our Lord, and to the good of the human race, they could not have done so more efficaciously than by what they did in their malice in bringing about the Passion.

Thus the Apostle, as we may say, draws out the thoughts of the *Magnificat*, and there is scarcely anything in his glowing language which is not founded on these simple words of Mary.

The other words of the passage on which we are engaged put the same great act of God's mercy in another light. It is no longer the humiliation of the proud and the elevation of the humble, but it is the filling of the hungry with good things and sending away empty the rich. Our Lady must be thought to apply this image in the same way as the former, to the mystery of the Incarnation. Her words are so few and so pregnant in their meaning that we must suppose that every one of them must be studied singly. This passage in the *Magnificat* contains at least three principles, each of which may be considered as something distinct from the rest. In the third place, she says that He fills the hungry with good things and sends away empty the rich. She seems to speak of the same classes of the creatures of God under several names, first of the proud, the mighty and the rich, and then of the humble or lowly, and the hungry who are filled. She seems to refer in each of these clauses to the evil angels on the one hand and to the race of men elevated by the Incarnation on the other.

We trace here the presence of the thought of the enmities which God was to place from the beginning between the promised mother and Satan, and between his seed and hers, although her mind is too calm to admit of any personal triumph, and she dwells exclusively on the divine action in her own exaltation.

We come now to the last portion of this canticle. In this, Our Lady speaks of one more of the great attributes of God as manifested in the work of the Incarnation. This is the attribute of His wonderful and most patient faithfulness. "He hath received Israel His servant, being mindful of His mercy (as He spoke to our fathers), to Abraham and his seed for ever." Thus there are three stages of this faithfulness of God. The act is one thing, the remembrance of mercy is another thing, and the accomplishment of the promise is another thing. All these are commemorated singly and specially by Our Lady in these words.

The word which is used for what is "received" is a word kindred to that used by St. Paul when he speaks of the Incarnation in the Epistle to the Hebrews. There he says, "Nowhere doth He take hold of the Angels, but of the seed of Abraham He taketh hold."[5] It implies, in the thought of Our Lady, no

[5] Heb. ii. 16.

common kind of helping, or receiving, or choosing, but that taking hold of which the Apostle speaks when He dwells on the truth that God has made Himself Man of the seed of Abraham.[6] This then must be thought to be the meaning of Our Lady in this place to mention once again the supreme race and condescension of God in the Incarnation and then to go on to point out that the Incarnation was an instance not only of the power, and the holiness, and the mercifulness of God, but also of His faithfulness.

God might have become man by a new creation, as Adam, without father or mother. But it pleased Him to become Man in the way in which He did, by making one of His own creatures His mother. And it pleased Him to do this by choosing this blessed mother from a particular race and family, which He had pointed out from the earliest times as the object of His choice. He chose to promise what He was to perform, and to perform what He had promised, to show Himself not only merciful, but mindful, faithful, and not to be driven from redeeming His pledge and crowning the hopes which He had raised.

To Our Lady, whose mind was so full of the intelligence of the rights of God, and who knew also so well the miserable history of His treatment at the hands of the people which He had chosen for His own, this attribute of His faithfulness in His promises must have seemed more wonderful than it may seem to us. Perhaps in her own deep humility the close of her *Magnificat* may have had some reference to the last words of her cousin to herself, "Blessed thou that didst believe! because those things shall be accomplished which

---

6 Heb. ii. 16.

were spoken to thee by the Lord!" and she may have made it a subject of the purest joy in her own heart, that she had to be the instrument of the most beneficent counsel of Him Who was not only most mighty, most powerful, most holy, and most merciful, but also most faithful.

The large and simple lines of thought which are followed out in the *Magnificat* make it fit for that general and continual use by the Catholic Church for which it has been destined by God. Day after day, in her Vesper service, the Church lifts up the hymn of Mary as the fittest expression of her own dutiful affections, giving glory and thanks to God. She rejoices and gives thanks for the elevation of the Mother of God, for the glory which thence redounds to her God and her Son, and also for the immense benefits which make generation after generation eager to call her blessed. The elevation of Mary is the greatest fruit of the Incarnation, and when the Church rejoices over it, she sees in it all the elevation of all the saints and all the blessed by virtue of the Precious Blood. It is the highest expression of that principle of the kingdom of the Incarnation. Mary's privilege, like the prerogative of her Son, is unique, but it is reflected in the glory and the power of the saints of God.

The Church finds the rejoicing of Mary over the defeat of God's enemies the natural expression of her own gratitude for His endless mercies, and for the peculiar love and predilection with which He has looked in mercy on the race of Adam, and raised it, even after its Fall, to the thrones left vacant by the rebel angels.

Chapter X

THE NATIVITY OF ST. JOHN

St. Luke i. 59–80. Vita Vitæ Nostræ, § 7.

The Gospel narrative tells us nothing more about the Visitation of our Blessed Lady than that she remained at her cousin's house about three months and then returned to Nazareth. These three months, during which the visit of Our Lady certainly lasted, must have been a time of wonderful repose, prayer, spiritual profit, and close intercourse with God. Our Lord was present in the womb of His Blessed Mother in the house of Zachary, and His presence was known and honored, both by the Blessed Mother herself and by her hosts. For it is hard to suppose that St. Zachary did not share the divine knowledge with his wife and his child.

The presence of Our Lord with His Blessed Mother meant a perpetual stream of fresh graces and holiest inspirations to her soul. It meant a continual homage of affections of the most tender love and gratitude on her part to Him. We have seen what it effected in the souls of St. John and St. Elizabeth at the first moment when it began, and we shall see immediately its effects on the soul of St. Zachary himself. The period of these three months was a time of immense and most rapid spiritual growth, though, like many such times in the history of souls, it was outwardly a period unmarked by any great events which could attract attention.

"And Mary abode with her about three months, and she returned to her own house." It has been thought by some of the Christian commentators that these words imply that the visit of our Blessed Lady came to an end before the time for the birth of the child of St. Elizabeth. But it seems unsafe to argue peremptorily that our Blessed Lady was not present at the birth of St. John. It is evident that the narrative is cast in the form which it now bears for the sake of keeping more distinct the two mysteries, the mystery of the Visitation and the birth of St. John.

"Now Elisabeth's full time of being delivered was come, and she brought forth a son. And her neighbors and her kinsfolk heard that the Lord had showed His great mercy towards her, and they congratulated with her." The fact of the birth of a child at the natural time was nothing that could create wonder, but we are not told that St. Elizabeth had made her state of pregnancy known before the time came for her to become a mother indeed. It is said in the Gospel narrative that she hid herself for five months after her conception. But, in any case, the birth of a son was what had been predicted by the angel to her husband. The birth of a son was always considered a matter for special congratulation.

But a still greater marvel was immediately to take place. They were therefore prepared to receive with great astonishment the sudden and complete restoration of the gift of speech to St. Zachary. This was what now took place.

"And immediately his mouth was opened, and his tongue was loosed, and he spoke, blessing God." There was something prodigious about his conception, as was evident from the great age of his mother, there was something of a divine purpose in his coming into the world, as was evident from the circumstances which had occurred about his name, and there was also the wonder of the sudden recovery of his father from the affliction which had been so many months upon him.

"And fear came upon all their neighbors, and all these words were divulged," that is, spread abroad, "over all the mountainous country of Judea." The city in which St. Zachary dwelt was on the hills, which form a considerable part of the inheritance of the tribe of Juda. In such a country, report would easily fly from town to town. "And all they who had heard them laid them up in their heart, saying, What an one think ye, shall this child be? For the hand of the Lord was upon him."

The Annunciation and Visitation are mysteries of pure joy. We apply the name "joyous" to other parts of the Holy Infancy, such as the Nativity itself, the Purification, and the Finding in the Temple of the Holy Child. But in all these three mysteries, there is something of the shadow, indeed, of more than the shadow, of the cross, and other portions of the history are more distinctly marked with the brand of suffering. But it is not to be found in the Annunciation and in the Visitation. It is as if the good providence of God had chosen to give to our Blessed Lady at least these three months of unmixed joy.

Thus were fulfilled those words of St. Gabriel to St. Zachary that at the birth of St. John, many should rejoice. The presence of Our Lord in the womb of His Blessed Mother had wrought the most wonderful results in the souls of those aged saints and their still more blessed son.

Joy enlightens, and enlarges, and fortifies, and enriches in a marvelous manner and degree. Our Blessed Lady was already consummate in all perfection of virtue, and yet it may have been the will of God that she should have this season of intense and unalloyed rejoicing immediately after the accomplishment of the Incarnation in order that she might grow ever more mightily and swiftly in grace, and He may have had the same purpose with regard to the souls of St. John and of his parents. Few souls may be fit for the most intense and continual joy, which yet may be the most profitable of all the measures of grace to those who are already the furthest advanced in perfect union with Him Whose life is essentially joy, unceasing, unalloyed, unalterable, and ineffable in its brightness.

The *Benedictus* grows out of the *Magnificat,* singing the praises of God more especially for the fruits of the Incarnation.

Chapter XI

The Canticle of Zachary

St. Luke i. 67–80. Vita Vitæ Nostræ, § 7.

"And Zachary his father was filled with the Holy Ghost, and he prophesied."

"Blessed be the Lord God of Israel, because He hath visited and wrought the redemption of His people, and He hath raised up a horn of salvation for us in the house of David His servant." St. Zachary catches up the last strain in the song of our Blessed Lady. She had left out all reference to her own ancestor David. Now St. Zachary fills up the omission, speaking of God as the God of Israel but adding that He had raised up His servant David.

The redemption which He has wrought is not any temporal deliverance, such as those of the people from the bondage of Egypt, but the spiritual deliverance from the bondage of sin and Satan. This is the only true deliverance worthy of the condescension of the God of Israel, and unless we were to be delivered from these spiritual slaveries and enemies, all temporal prosperity would be of light account.

"He hath raised up a horn of salvation for us, in the house of His servant David." These words at once give the character of the Son of David to Our Lord and imply the fulfillment of all the special promises made about the throne of David. Our Lord is Savior and also King. The house of God's servant David is specially mentioned as the home of this great salvation. Thus the saint refers immediately to the words of the angel at the Annunciation about the "throne of David His father, and that He was to reign in the house of Jacob for ever, and that of His kingdom there was to be no end." This is the proper scriptural account of Our Lord's work, that He is not simply a Redeemer, but also a King, as St. Zachary says that God has raised up this horn of salvation because the family of David had for many centuries lost the royal power and dignity, and thus the kingdom had to be restored, a most true and spiritual kingdom.

Thus we find that the first line added by St. Zachary brings out two great features in the dispensation of the Incarnation. The first of these features is that it is distinctly a dispensation of redemption. Our Lady had left undescribed the kingdom of the Redemption; St. Zachary tells us that the visitation of the people of God is for the purpose of redemption.

He tells us in the second place that this redemption is enshrined in a visible kingdom, settled on the House of David. The Redeemer then, is a King, reigning, according to the words of St. Gabriel, forever in the House of Jacob, a King of whose kingdom there was to be no end.

"As He spoke by the mouth of His holy prophets who are from the beginning, salvation from our enemies, and from the hand of all who hate us. To perform mercy to our fathers, and to remember His holy testament, the oath which he swore to Abraham our father that he would grant us." St.

Zachary specially mentions the prophets who are from the beginning. This expression in Scripture seems to signify the great antiquity of those who are thus spoken of, but it may be taken literally in the present case. For prophecy is one of the institutions of God's government of the world which has been in operation from the very beginning, His words imply that the promise contained the grounds of hope resting on faith in the coming Redeemer, and that this faith embraced the remission of sins and spiritual reconciliation. But this was in a special way the characteristic of the promise by which enmities were set between the woman and the serpent, and her Seed and his seed. The words of the canticle, therefore, imply that the promise of the remission of sins was made at the very beginning.

St. Zachary goes on, in the verses which immediately follow, to describe this kingdom by a twofold note. The characteristic of a well-ordered and flourishing kingdom is, in the first place, its security from outward danger and aggression. This was one great element in the prosperity of the kingdom under Solomon. The other characteristic of a kingdom in a happy state is that there is internal peace and freedom from everything that may breed division. It seems as if the holy father of the Baptist intended to describe the kingdom of which he speaks as distinguished in both these ways. He first speaks of "salvation from our enemies, and from the hand of all that hate us," and then he goes on to add the other characteristic note "that we being delivered out of the hand of our enemies might serve Him without fear, in holiness and justice before Him all the days of our life." Thus the promised kingdom is described as possessing the great characteristics of the highest prosperity, external and internal alike.

"Salvation from our enemies and from the hand of all that hate us." We may well understand the words as promising us deliverance from the dangers which beset us from enemies like our own sensuality, the flesh, and the world, and in the second place, from enemies who are full of the most venomous and relentless hatred of us. Thus we are promised deliverance from these two kinds of foes, internal and external, according to that passage of St. Paul, where he says that "our wrestling is not against flesh and blood," meaning not only against our own sensuality, "but against principalities and powers,"[1] and the rest. Not that we are to be delivered from the assaults of the flesh and the corruption within us, or of the devils and their agents outside us, but that the merits of the redemption are sufficient to give us strength to make these assaults the occasions of victory and triumph.

"To perform mercy to our fathers, and to remember His holy testament, the oath which He swore to our father Abraham, that He would give us." In these words, it does not seem fanciful to discern a kind of reference to the names of the holy family in which this beautiful canticle had its origin. For the name of John signifies the grace or the mercy of God, and the name Zachary signifies the memory of God, and the name Elizabeth signifies the oath of God. The name of John had been specially given by the angel at the time of the revelation to Zachary of the miraculous conception which was to take place, and it had been insisted on specially

1 Ephes. Vi. 12.

by both the parents when he had to be named at his circumcision. Having thus begun to apply the meaning of the name of the child, it was natural to go on with the allusions to his own name and the name of his wife. The testament, or covenant, of which the saint speaks may be understood generally of all the promises of God.

But the more precise meaning of the word may be that which applies it to the covenant made with Abraham of which the rite of circumcision was the appointed sign. There is here a kind of advance and increase in the faithfulness of God. He was bound to perform mercy to the fathers, first because He was, as St. Peter calls Him, a faithful Creator, Who would not therefore forget His children in their need. He was bound also by His special promises, and particularly by the promise which He had given when the covenant of circumcision was made with Abraham and his race. They had the special privilege of being in covenant with God, a privilege sealed to them by the sacred rite of circumcision, which had just been performed for the infant son of St. Zachary. They had the still further assurance, on which St. Paul thinks it well to insist, of the oath of God made to Abraham, after he had shown his faithfulness in not withholding from God even his only son, in whom the promises made to him were bound up. And finally, the act of Abraham was a foreshadowing of the act of God in giving to us His own Son.

The next words of the canticle set forth the substance of the great promise, of the covenant, of the oath, the effects and fruits of the gift of the horn of salvation raised up in the house of David. "That He would grant to us that being delivered from the hand of our enemies we may serve Him without fear, in holiness and justice before Him all our days." This, then, is the boon conferred on men by the Incarnation in the kingdom of Christ. We are delivered from the hand of our enemies, and we can serve Him in holiness and justice before Him, without fear, and this all our days. These words may be considered as summing up the fundamental privileges of the Gospel dispensation. In the first place, the grace of God delivers us from the hand of those enemies. We have already pointed out that this twofold description seems to cover the chief requirements of a peaceful and flourishing kingdom. Here they appear rather as the malignant assailants of mankind than as the rebels against God in His own kingdom. We are delivered from their power, not by being altogether removed from the reach of their attacks, but by being strengthened against them after having been set free from the kind of slavery in which men were held by them before the Gospel privileges were brought home to them.

The fear of which St. Zachary speaks was the fear characteristic of the Law, a servile fear, and as such, a thing to be changed for the free loving service and reverential fear of the children. Thus St. Paul says, "You have not received the spirit of bondage again in fear, but you have received the spirit of adoption of sons whereby we cry, Abba Father."[2] Again, the justice and holiness of the Gospel dispensation are far superior to anything that could be ordinarily attained under the Law. For the Gospel graces enable men to practice lofty virtues and live a life which is truly a participation of the divine life, as St. John says that God has given us so

---

2 Romans viii. 15.

much charity[3] that we are called and are the sons of God, and St. Peter speaks of Christians as being made partakers of the Divine Nature.[4] The justice or virtue which can be reached under the Gospel are truly such, and most heavenly in their perfection.

The saint then adds the two particular blessings which crown this gift of holiness and justice, namely, that these perfections are practiced by Christians before God. By this he may mean either that they are truly such virtues as to be esteemed as such by God Himself, or he may mean that the Gospel state of the service of God is a kind of life in His presence, a close familiarity with Him which was unattainable before. This is because Our Lord really lives in us, as He says in the discourse in which He promises the Blessed Eucharist, and also because that great mystery itself makes our God present to us in a new way which had no parallel in the older covenant. Finally, the last words of this clause, "all our days," may be considered as involving the gift of perseverance, which is comparatively easier under the Gospel dispensation.

This, then, is the substance of the divine promise to the Fathers, as explained by the blessed Zachary in his canticle. Our enemies, who hate us with an inveterate and most intense hatred, because we are God's creatures and highly favored by Him, are checked and beaten off, their tyrannical power over us is destroyed, and we are fortified against them, not only by the weakening of their forces but by the strengthening of our own.

---

3 I St. John iii. 1.

4 2 Peter i. 4.

We may now pass on to the second part of this canticle. Next he turns to his own child and speaks to him of the glorious commission which he was to receive in the preparation of this new kingdom. "And thou, child, shalt be called the prophet of the Highest, for thou shalt go before the face of the Lord to prepare His way. To give knowledge of salvation to His people unto the remission of their sins, through the bowels of the mercy of our God, in which the Orient from on high hath visited us, to enlighten them that sit in darkness and in the shadow of death, to direct our feet into the way of peace."

The first words of the hymn are a kind of paraphrase of the words of the angel to St. Zachary himself. St. Gabriel had said, "He shall go before Him in the spirit and power of Elias, that he may turn the hearts of the fathers unto the children, and the incredulous to the wisdom of the just, to prepare unto the Lord a perfect people." St. Zachary understood this commission of his holy child. He was to be the prophet of the Highest. The Highest Himself then was to come, He was already among them, He had visited them, but St. John was to go before His face, and was to be called His prophet. He was to be His precursor.

He was to proclaim His near approach. He was to fit the people for receiving Him when He came, especially by his preaching of repentance. For repentance was the one indispensable condition to enable men to receive Our Lord when He came, because His mission was one for the remission of sins. And when he had prepared the people to receive Our Lord by the preaching of repentance, by the baptism which was a profession of the state of penitence, then he was to reveal Our Lord personally to them by pointing Him out. In these many ways, St. John was to be a prophet, and as Our Lord said of him, more than a prophet. He left behind him no prediction, he worked no miracle. His prediction was the pointing out a Person already among them. His miracles were the penitence and the conversion to which he roused the people.

St. Zachary goes on to describe the substance of the message which his son was to deliver. "To give knowledge of salvation unto His people, unto the remission of their sins." The words "knowledge of salvation" may contain another allusion to the holy name of Jesus, as if it were meant that St. John was to make known to the people that salvation was now brought home to them by the advent of Our Lord and the preaching of His kingdom. The two things which Our Lord lays down as conditions of salvation are faith and repentance, which is included in baptism. His words when He began to preach were, "the kingdom of heaven is at hand, do penance and believe the Gospel." After the institution of baptism, He said, "he that believeth and is baptized shall be saved, he that believeth not shall be condemned." The salvation made known by St. John was thus the repentance from sin and the faith in Jesus Christ. This is what his father here says about giving knowledge of salvation to the people unto the remission of their sins. St. John was sent to make known Our Lord as the object of faith, the Redeemer, the Lamb of God Who taketh away the sin of the world, and thus his mission is most accurately described in the words of this canticle.

"Through the bowels of the mercy of our God, in which the Orient from on high hath visited us." That is, as it seems, the remission of our sins through Jesus Christ is above all to be traced up to the compassionate love of God for us as its original fountain head and source. It was not simple compassion, but compassion set in motion and urged on to its wonderful excesses by the most tender love for us on the part of God. There was nothing in us by way of merit to bring down on us the mercy of God in the Incarnation. It was all because He loved us so much even while we were His enemies. It is to this original fountain of love that the blessed Zachary traces the condescension of the Incarnation and of the redemption wrought thereby. For it is in those bowels of mercy that he says that the Orient from on high hath visited us, using once again the word which refers to the presence of Our Lord in the womb of His Blessed Mother in the humble dwelling of himself and St. Elizabeth. That is, he refers to the Incarnation as the special fruit of this combination of love and of compassion. God might have had mercy on us in a thousand ways. But the way He chose was the way of this visitation, for love is not content with mercy. It must share itself the low condition of those whom it loves, and this issued in God becoming man, thus making Himself poor and carrying out His mercy in that way rather than in any other.

The word in the original, which is rendered here "the Orient," or the dayspring, is in the Greek a word which primarily conveys the idea of springing up, and may be applied to anything that can be said to spring up. Of these things there are two of which the word is used in Sacred Scripture. These are the light of the dawning day, which shoots up through the darkness overhead, and the shoot or branch of a tree. Either image might be represented by the Greek word. The holy author of the canticle did not probably mean to quote directly any one of the many passages when he used the word.

It may perhaps be said, in explanation of the use of this twofold image, that the truth which the image represents requires both comparisons to represent it fully. The image of a plant springing up, a branch growing and expanding, is admirably suited to represent the gradual progress, whether of Our Lord Himself in His manifestations in the Incarnation or of the kingdom which He came to found. Such an image is required for the economy of the Incarnation. On the other hand, the dawning of light is not a gradual growth. It is, rather, a sudden burst of glory, chasing away the shadows and darkness of night.

But the idea in the mind of Zachary is, first of all, God visiting His people in His own Person. He comes down from on high first and then manifests Himself gradually when He has come down. The dayspring visiting from on high is the first part of the Incarnation; the shoot springing up from the ground is the second, the gradual revelation of the Incarnate Son.

"To enlighten them that sit in darkness and in the shadow of death, to direct our feet into the way of peace." Thus does the blessed Zachary sum up the ends and effects of this visitation of the dayspring from on high. The first effect is the dispelling of darkness, and the second effect is the guiding into the way of peace. The whole world, Jews as well as heathens, were sitting helpless in darkness and in the shadow of death. The image of sitting implies that they were making no effort to relieve themselves. They were powerless and hopeless. The desire of the world for God is expressed in the beautiful image used by St. Paul in his address at the Areopagus at Athens, where he says that God had set all the nations of the earth "that they should seek God, if happily they may feel after Him, or find Him," using a word which describes the groping of men in the dark after the way, or the door, or whatever they need. And in his former speech at Lystra, the Apostle had said that God, though He "suffered all nations to walk in their own ways, nevertheless left not Himself without testimony doing good from heaven, giving rains and fruitful seasons, filling our hearts with food and gladness."[5]

But to sit in darkness is, as it were, to give up the search after God, notwithstanding the many instincts and needs of nature which were always prompting men to seek after Him, as we see in the history of the philosophy of the Greeks. At the time of Our Lord, all the world is described as sitting hopeless and helpless. The Jews had the sacred traditions and the truth about God; they knew what they worshipped, as Our Lord said, but they were in darkness and the shadow of death, the former on account of their great ignorance, and the latter on account of their many dominant sins. The Gentiles were in far greater ignorance of God than the Jews, because they not only knew Him not, but they served the devil and their own lusts under the names of a number of false deities,

---

[5] Acts xvii. 27, xiv. 16.

whose worship was connected with intense moral degradation. Thus even the moral law had become largely obscured among them, as it is now among many nations outside the Christian pale. And thus their ignorance was united to the shadow of death, which is the special image of sin, as distinguished from ignorance, to a degree which was not to be found among the chosen people.

But now, for both of these, the dawn from heaven was shooting far up into the sky to enlighten both, the Jews first and through them the Gentiles, and the other blessed effect was soon to follow on or accompany the dispelling of the darkness, the guiding of their feet into the way of true peace, to enable them to reconcile themselves with God and thus enjoy peace of conscience, to know Him and Jesus Christ whom He had sent, to understand His commandments, to be able to obey them, to wield the whole armament of grace and light which was to be provided for them in the teaching and sacraments of the Church. This may be sufficient as a commentary on these beautiful and soothing words. But they may perhaps also include reference to that peace of which St. Paul speaks more than once, the taking away the wall of division between different peoples among the children of God and the foundation of the one Church in which all are to be one.

"And the child grew, and was strengthened in spirit, and was in the deserts until the day of his manifestation unto Israel." These few words sum up all that we are told, on the authority of Scripture, concerning the infancy and early manhood of St. John. Here, again, is a time of silence into which we should be glad to peer, if it was in our power. For the childhood of the saints of God is often very full of wonders and anticipations of their future services to God. In the case of St. John, there would probably be many unusually wonderful manifestations of sanctity in his earliest years as well as later on. We are only told that he grew in body and that, as he advanced in years, the Spirit of God within him grew stronger and stronger. In his case, there was a real continual advance in grace, as there had also been in our Blessed Lady. The other thing which we are told of St. John is that he was in the deserts until the time came for him to come forth to the world as a preacher of penitence. It is likely that his parents may have died not many years after his birth, and the marvelous child may have then taken up his abode as a hermit in the desert, preparing, by continual prayer and intercourse with God and the practice of mortification and silence, for the great work which was to be committed to him.

Chapter XII

THE TRIAL OF ST. JOSEPH

St. Matt. i. 18–25. Vita Vitæ Nostræ, § 6.

We may proceed to draw out the hidden history of this great saint during the interval between the Incarnation and the incident which St. Matthew has here related of the vision in which the angel appeared to him in his sleep. Holy Scripture is enough for us because it says so few things about these treasures of the secret action of God; it by no means follows that it tells us nothing or even little in those few words.

If St. Joseph had been absent from his wife during the greater part of these three months, it might be supposed that even naturally he would become aware of the pregnancy of Our Lady on his return to her side.

Here we are met by a considerable difference of opinion among the Catholic commentators. We have reason for thinking that both Our Lady and her husband were bound to maintain the most perfect continence in their married state, that St. Joseph was conscious of and a consenting party to the vow of virginity of which Our Lady had spoken to the angel at the time of the Annunciation, and that he was himself a partner in that holy resolution.

But the incidents of that wonderful time were mainly interior. The greatest thing that had ever happened in the history of creation had taken place in silence, when the Eternal Word of God became Man in the womb of Mary. Then began that marvelous existence of the Word made Flesh, which was from that moment the chief delight of the Eternal Father. Then began the life of the Sacred Heart, with all its rich fruits of the most beautiful and intense acts of virtue. Then began that close companionship between the Heart of the Son and the heart of the mother, which, next to the communing with God of the Sacred Heart Itself, was the most wonderful and glorious thing in the spiritual world that had ever been in existence. Then began with fresh impetuosity and intensity that ever-increasing perfection of the interior life of Mary, open only to God in its fullness, but to some extent revealed to the celestial citizens, which, next to the human life of Our Lord, was the most precious thing that earth had ever produced, or ever could produce, in the sight of its Maker. As each day passed over the head of Mary and of the Divine Babe in her womb, it gave occasion to the most beautiful worship and obedience to God that had ever been rendered, and the prayers and affections of these two Sacred Hearts rose up in a perpetual column of incense, so to say, before the Throne on high.

Even if we suppose that St. Joseph had no part in the divine secret at first, it does not follow that he too was not at this time an object of the highest pleasure to God on account of the manner in which he bore himself under the new circumstances in which the Holy Family was placed. God derived great glory from the homage paid to our Blessed Lady by her cousin St. Elizabeth. He was greatly glorified by the exultation of the holy Baptist in the womb of his mother. It is not much to think that at this same time God was receiving the homage of very noble and precious virtues from the pure and humble soul of the holy spouse of Mary. We have already said that the fact that no revelation had been directly made to St. Joseph, at the time of the Incarnation does not of itself prove that he had no other knowledge or surmise of what had taken place.

It is at this point that it seems most natural to suppose that the hesitation and trial of St. Joseph took place.

But something more must be added before we are able to look at this question with perfect clearness. What has hitherto been said supposes that the hesitation or doubt of St. Joseph would have been entirely removed if he had at once had a divine certainty concerning the truth of the Divine Conception. This is far from being the case. That the Child of Mary was divinely conceived by the operation of the Holy Ghost was one truth, and that St. Joseph was to perform for Him the part of a father was quite another. It must be remembered that no amount of certainty on the first point could shed any light upon the second. God might have chosen Mary for His mother without choosing Joseph for His earthly father and protector.

But this was preeminently a point as to which a certain guidance from heaven was necessary. Moreover, the inspiration under which Mary had acted in going to visit St. Elizabeth was given to her and not to her husband. She must have submitted it to him as her own thought. After the revelation to St. Joseph, all the movements of the Holy Family are made in consequence of revelations to him and not to her. But this method of the divine guidance had not yet begun.

Thus, even if we were quite certain that St. Joseph knew the mystery of the Incarnation as fully as, or more fully than, St. Elizabeth and St. Zachary, the further question whether he was to assume any position of authority or protection over the divinely chosen mother remained perfectly unsolved until the time came for God to solve it. We may now return to the simple words of the Evangelist with which we are dealing.

The Scripture narrative informs us that when he found that Mary was with child by the Holy Ghost, St. Joseph did not know at once what it was right for him to do. He was a just man and therefore did not wish to expose her to any public discredit. It was thus that he conceived the half-formed resolution of "putting her away privately."

Though St. Matthew has not thought it his business to explain exactly which of several alternatives is the true one in fact, yet it is fair to think that here, as in other places in his Gospel, where his great brevity have left a difficulty for his readers, he has been at some pains to give them a hint as to the solution of that difficulty. In this place, we consider that he has left such a hint in the words "she was found to be with child of the Holy Ghost." These words seem to imply that he who found her with child—that is, St. Joseph—knew that the Child was conceived by the Holy Ghost. Let us see what are the possible states of mind which are consistent with the language of St. Matthew with regard to St. Joseph. These possibilities will be found to correspond to the various interpretations which are adopted by the Fathers as to the words before us.

It is possible, in the first place, that St. Matthew may mean that St. Joseph found that his wife was with child but did not know the secret of the conception by the Holy Ghost. In this case, the words "by the Holy Ghost" are added by the Evangelist, as it were, before their time, probably for the sake of not waiting a single moment without a protest in favor of the truth, and for the more perfect honor of the Blessed Mother. This state of mind, however, might admit of various phases of opinion or surmise or conjecture or decided judgment. St. Joseph probably knew that the Messias was to be born of a pure virgin, in some marvelous way, without having any clear idea of the manner in which His conception was to be brought about, whether it was to be by the direct action of the Holy Ghost or whether some supernatural power was to enable her to conceive without any other agency than her own. The prophets had said nothing about the action of the Holy Ghost. St. Joseph might have surmised that something marvelous had taken place, but he would have no suspicion or fear of anything that could be blameworthy in Mary.

We must add a second hypothesis for the sake of exhausting the possibilities of the case—that he might have had some undefined fear, which did not amount to a certain judgment, that she had in some way which he could not conjecture, or explain, conceived in the natural manner. But it seems inconsistent with the character of this glorious saint, as well as with the knowledge which he must have had of the holiness of his wife and of her vow of virginity, that he could have formed the thought that she could have violated her vow and that she was to blame and worthy of dismissal from his home on the one ground on which Our Lord afterward allowed separation.

In the next place, if it be asked what is meant, in accordance with this supposition, by the fear of St. Joseph and his resolution or design of putting Our Lady away in private, we can only think that he meant to withdraw in some manner from her company, perhaps leaving the place of his abode for some place unknown so that it might not be obvious that he had entirely and forever left her to herself. His fear would be that of living any longer with her, and this fear, in the hypothesis before us, would be simply grounded on his ignorance of the manner of her conception. He was not reproached for his fear by St. Gabriel, as Zachary had been blamed for his slowness of faith. He was bidden by the angel to have no fear of "taking to himself" his wife, and he is said after the vision to have "taken to himself" his wife.

The words of the Evangelist are equally consistent with other suppositions as to the state of mind of St. Joseph. They are consistent with the supposition which is suggested by St. Jerome in the lesson which the Church has selected to be read on Christmas Eve. This is, that seeing her to be with child by the Holy Ghost, he did not think that it was for him, without further authority, to act as her husband in the bringing up of the Child to which she was to give birth, and that therefore he thought it well to retire and leave the work of God to His own good providence. This hypothesis makes St. Joseph fully conscious of the divine mystery but afraid to mix himself up with its execution without authority. It is not easy to exaggerate the importance of the difficulty which is here supposed to have weighed with this blessed Father but which is so often left unconsidered by writers on the Gospels.

It surely might well appear most presumptuous on the part of one in his position to seem, to the eyes of the world, to be the Father of the Divine Child, unless it were quite certain that it was the will of God that so it should be. It might even seem to St. Joseph a kind of sacrilege to present himself to the world in such a light. He might have seen something of those reasons of theological convenience in this divine arrangement, after it was made, which are dwelt on by the Fathers of the Church in their explanations of this passage. That is one thing. But it would have been quite another to assume without authority that he might act as to give to the world the impression that the Divine Child was his own son. It might have seemed to him that such a course might be bearing a false witness in this great economy of the Incarnation and giving to future enemies of the truth a ground for denying the very divinity of Our Lord. It may be considered as absolutely impossible that St. Joseph, with all his humility and spiritual discernment, could have thus thrust himself into the mystery of which not a word had yet been said to him on the part of God.

It is this hypothesis which seems to be the most reasonable explanation of the history before us. It seems almost impossible to think that, however certain St. Joseph might have felt that his holy spouse was in truth the mother of the promised Messias, the virgin spoken of in the prophecy of Isaias and in those of Jeremias and Micheas, as well as in other predictions of the redemption of the world, he could not have gone on acting as the father of her Child without a special divine commission so to act. If it had been possible for him to have been present at the Annunciation as at the Visitation, if he had received from Mary herself the full narrative of all that had passed in her, if St. Elizabeth had told him all that she knew by divine revelation of the mystery of the Incarnation, still until the words of the angel to himself, bidding him act as he was to act, it does not seem possible to think that he could have taken on him the office which God intended for him without having that office specially conferred upon him. Nothing had been said to Mary, nothing had been said to Elizabeth, nowhere was it written in the prophecies that he, as the husband of Mary, was to take the place of the father of the Incarnate God. But the relation in which St. Joseph was to stand to Our Lord was to be so unique that it naturally required nothing short of a revelation to establish it.

It is, moreover, not difficult to see that the delay in this revelation to St. Joseph may have served many purposes in the order of Providence. For it enabled him to be tested by God as to his fidelity before he assumed the great office destined for him. We conclude then with perfect confidence that the perplexity of St. Joseph was not about his wife's condition but about his own conduct considering that condition. It was not whether Mary had conceived by the Holy Ghost but how he was to act in consequence of her divine conception.

We may turn from these considerations to that of the very beautiful and glorious virtues which must have been exercised by St. Joseph under this providential trial. St. Joseph could not but know that the mother of the Messias was to be a pure virgin, and it would not have been beyond the reach of supernatural charity that he might have said to himself that he would rather believe that the great miracle had taken place in her than form a judgment adverse to her in his own mind.

He could not have obeyed the angel's commands with more unquestioning docility. But the truth which the angel revealed to St. Joseph was no less a marvel than the miraculous conception of the Son of God in the womb of a pure virgin. And the injunction which was conveyed to him at the same time was no less than a command to act for the rest of his life as the father of that Incarnate God.

Again, even though a saint, it might have been expected that he would have asked for some sign, or have made some difficulty, as Zachary did. But instead of this, he is perfectly satisfied with the simple intimation of the truth and of the will of God given in a dream. We cannot help seeing how full he must have been of true spiritual discernment, how ready to believe great things of God, how well instructed in the prophecies, and at the same time how wonderfully full of the deepest and truest humility so as to shrink with all his heart from the great position, which some men might have claimed without further doubt, of the head of the family of which the other members were Jesus and Mary. He did not grasp or clutch at this honor when it seemed to be within his reach, as it is implied by St. Paul of Satan, that he clutched eagerly at what seemed to him to be a chance of being equal with God. With the simplest and deepest humility, St. Joseph thinks of hiding his own unworthiness in flight. But by that very reluctance, he made himself all the more worthy to be as the father of the Child.

His humility led him so far, and then there came the command of God, another call on his humility in the form of the most immediate and unhesitating docility, and the whole of the beautiful history of the Holy Family became possible because the father of the family was there as well as the mother and the Child. There would have been a great gap in the holy home of Nazareth if it had been otherwise. And if there had been a page in that beautiful history left unwritten, so also would there have been left unwritten a most beautiful and glorious page in the history of the Catholic Church in heaven and on earth. We should have missed all the prodigies of love and power contained in the exercise of the patronage of St. Joseph. Just as the humility and the purity of our Blessed Lady were the divinely appointed foundations of her dignity as the Mother of God, so on the docility and the humility and the charity of St. Joseph were to be built the other great virtues, the beauties of which his presidency of the Holy Family unfolded before God and the angels.

In the first place, it appears fairly certain that, though absent from the side of Mary during the greater part of the three months, he must have accompanied her to the house of her cousin, and have come back, at the time of the circumcision of St. John, to fetch her again to their home. This implies that he must almost certainly have heard his blessed spouse utter the *Magnificat*, and that he was probably present while Zachary carried on the strain of thanksgiving in his own glorious canticle. Now if this was so, it is not easy to see how the truth of the Incarnation in all its fullness could have been hidden from him. How could such strains as these ring on the ears of anyone even moderately conversant with the prophecies and the ways of God without awakening or intensifying the thought that the great mystery of the Incarnation had been accomplished in Mary? If the whole household of Zachary were living in this atmosphere of grateful glorification of God for His mercies, it is easy to suppose that it was also breathed by the blessed spouse of Mary.

We are in the habit of speaking of St. Joseph as the foster father, the putative father, and the like, of Our Lord. These expressions are rightly used of him, because in the ordinary sense of the word, Our Lord had no father on earth. But it must not be forgotten that, as St. Joseph had all the rights of a husband over our Blessed Lady, so had he all the authority and rights of a father over her Child, as soon as it was settled by a distinct decree of God that he was to discharge to each his natural office as the head of the Holy Family.

We may say just the same as to the great position of St. Joseph in the spiritual kingdom. Here also that position is secured by the trial through which he had passed. We are accustomed in the Church to venerate and have recourse to this great saint as having in a special manner the gift of guiding souls in spiritual perplexities and in the exercises of the interior life. But it is a law of God's providence that the saints who have special powers and offices of this kind are those who have themselves passed through the experience of the dangers and trials out of which they are able to help others to make their way in safety. In this way, the office of St. Joseph in the spiritual kingdom is founded on the experience of his own soul, and his power is the reward and fruit of his own faithfulness.

The experiences of the spiritual life are sometimes acquired in a long course of time; sometimes they are gained in a few hours into which are contracted the pains and the anguish of years. It may well have been so with St. Joseph. His trial was in itself unique and cannot ever be in all its features the trial of any one else. But it may well have included in itself a very deep and penetrating experience, and it may have been the providential preparation of his soul for the great office which he was to fulfill in the spiritual kingdom. One short period of trial and disturbance may often add more to the spiritual enlightenment of a soul in the path of perfection than many long periods of comparative tranquility and peace.

A further noticeable element in the providential arrangement of this epoch in the history of the Holy Family may be found in the new relation in which it placed these two most beautiful souls of Mary and Joseph one to the other, as well as in the intimate communion which must so soon have sprung up between the soul of the appointed father and that of the Divine Son in the womb of Mary. Very beautiful indeed must have been the relations between Joseph and Mary before the Incarnation. As far as earth went, they were all in all one to the other, and they were souls of the most transcendent sanctity and, on that account, souls between whom the most tender and perfect union could be formed. It is reasonable to believe that between souls that are very closely united to God even here, there may sometimes be the anticipation of the perfect openness and communion of the kingdom of bliss. And if ever there were two souls of whom this might be thought to be the case, those two souls would have certainly been the souls of Mary and of Joseph.

That which had come between them was not so much a cloud of misunderstanding as a threat of separation. Mary had been most wonderfully elevated, and the immensity of her dignity was enough in itself to place a distance between her and all the world. We see how this dignity of the Mother of God was recognized at once by the blessed Elizabeth. It is not easy to think that it was not recognized with equal veneration by St. Joseph himself. Up to this time, during the short period of their married life, there had not only been between them the closest union of hearts and purposes but there had been the most beautiful exercise of their mutual duties, the guidance and ruling of the husband and the obedience and reverence of the wife. And now she had become the Mother of God, and there had been no word of intimation from heaven whether this was to interfere with the relations which had hitherto existed between them. The elevation of the Blessed Virgin thus raised questions which must sooner or later be settled, and which cause a certain kind of perplexity.

And then, in God's good time, there came the blessed moment when all shadows were chased away by the message of the angel to St. Joseph, which determined his position in the new kingdom as plainly as the former message at the Annunciation had determined that of Mary herself. It was not a mere removal of doubt. It was the elevation of St. Joseph, as the Annunciation had been the elevation of Mary. It was the bestowal on him of a dignity second only to hers. There was to be no separation. The bond which God had once made fast was not to be unloosed. Their union was made more than ever indissoluble. If Mary was to become a mother, Joseph was to become as a father. The new bond of union between them was nothing less than the presence of the Incarnate Son of God, the Child of Mary. St. Joseph was to "take to himself" his wife. Their union was consecrated, not divided. He had a new office both to her and to her Child. She could see in him, not simply the spouse who was to be the guardian of her virgin purity, but the guide, and head, and provider of the Holy Family, now made complete and perfect by the presence of the Divine Infant in her womb.

What must have been the beauty and sublimity of their mutual converse as soon as Mary could speak without reserve to Joseph as to the great mystery which had taken place! However great we may imagine the pain to have been which may have fallen on these two tender souls during the time of darkness, such as it was, it is certain that far greater in proportion must have been the joy and delight of their reunion and the happiness which must have inundated them when each could see in the other an appointed instrument for the execution of the greatest work that God could do, and know that in this great work they were to labor side by side.

It is only natural to add to these thoughts the consideration of the immense new graces which must have come down both on our Blessed Lady and on St. Joseph after the completion of the trial. It is the way of God to delay the bestowal of His favors in order that those on whom they are to be conferred may be prepared for them in His providence, especially by the discipline of adversity and the exercise on their own parts of patience, humility, and other virtues. This principle runs through the whole of the sacred history, and it certainly had its place in the providential dealings of God with St. Joseph and our Blessed Lady.

Lastly, we may see in this mystery a great instance of what is continually taking place in the dealings of God with His saints. It is not the way of God in His ordinary dealings with His faithful servants to let them see beforehand what it is that they are to do for Him; it is not the common way with God to let the saints see what it is that is before them, either in the way of joy or in the way of suffering. Joseph and Mary had perhaps planned out a life for themselves. They might have intended to live a hidden life in their own quiet town, a life known only to God.

This would have been very beautiful, but the dreams, even of saints, are not so beautiful as the realities which God prepares for them in His providence, for His thoughts are not as ours. Now they were to change all their plans and to enter on a new and most marvelous career, a career full of the most terrible crosses as of the most heavenly delights. How far above all their conceptions was the path which God had marked out for them! How utterly different, and yet how much more splendid, the thoughts of God for them than their thoughts for themselves! And finally, if we ask what was the one foundation on which all this great edifice of sanctity was to be raised both in the one and in the other, we can find no other answer than that which Our Lady uttered in her *Magnificat—Quia respexit humilitatem ancillæ suæ*. The trial of Mary was one, and the trial of Joseph was another. But the virtue which raised them both to the thrones prepared for them was the same, the virtue of humility.

Chapter XIII

The Expectation of the Nativity

St. Luke ii. 1–15. Vita Vitæ Nostræ, § 8.

If we suppose the Incarnation to have taken place on the day which we now keep as the feast of the Annunciation, it seems naturally to follow that the end of the visit of our Blessed Lady to her cousin St. Elizabeth is to be fixed at the beginning of July. That would leave a space of between five and six months before the nativity of Our Lord Himself. Further, if we are right in thinking that the revelation as to the mystery of the Incarnation was made to St. Joseph just after the visitation of Our Lady, we have this space of something more than five months, of which no account is given us in the Gospels, but during which St. Joseph and our Blessed Lady were living together in the utmost happiness at Nazareth in preparation for the moment when the greatest event in the world's history was to take place in the birth of Our Lord.

There are blank spaces in our maps of the heavens, spaces in which there are no stars on which human eyes can gaze, even with the aid of the most powerful instruments. But it would be foolish for us to think that because our powers are limited, therefore it is certain that there are not many bodies of great magnitude and brilliancy to those who can discern them. Few of us think much of those five or six months in the existence of Jesus, Mary, and Joseph. And yet it cannot be doubted that every moment of this space of time was filled up by each of them with actions and affections most delightful and most glorious to God. It was a time of the deepest peace, the most perfect silence, the most fervent occupations and love, a time, the records of which, as far as they were manifested to the eager eyes of the angels, must have opened to them wonders of the divine condescension and wisdom such as they had never before conceived. The world went on as usual outside that sacred home, which was now the sanctuary of the Incarnate Lord.

The first thing that must strike us in our considerations of this wonderful time is the presence of God on earth in a new way, brought about by His union with our nature in that sacred humanity which was never from that moment to be separated from Him. To do honor to that special presence of God in which He vouchsafed to dwell with His chosen people, there had been ordained a Tabernacle on which the tribes of Israel had lavished all their treasures, and certain families had been set aside by a special consecration for His service there. There, by a whole elaborate system of holy rites and sacrifices, by continual praises and propitiations, honor had been done to Him. The Holy of Holies, in which the Ark of the Covenant was kept, was open to no one but the high priest alone once in the year. Later on, the Temple had been built by Solomon, and no holy place on earth was enriched so munificently, or guarded so reverently, no place ever drew to itself the homage and devotion of the most enlightened and holy among men. But now that He had really come upon earth, now that the Word had become Flesh, and "tabernacled" among men, the temple in which He was enshrined was nothing but the Sacred Body and Soul of Jesus Christ in the womb of Mary. There was that awful Presence around which is gathered the trembling adoration of the angelic host, there was its shrine, its temple, its throne, and it had no earthly worshippers but Mary and Joseph.

Another consideration that strikes us on this subject is that of the immense spiritual gifts which this Divine Presence would shed around it. Many indeed may the gifts have been which fell on the unconscious neighbors and friends of the parents of Our Lord. But the gifts of sanctification are usually by far the greatest to those who can best understand them and who can best correspond to them by their own cooperation.

Who, then, can be surprised at anything that the saints have said about the heights of holiness to which our Blessed Lady and her spouse were raised during this period of their silent dwelling with Our Lord? They were dwelling, as it were, in heaven itself, for they had Him with them Whose presence makes heaven what it is. Mary was, in truth, the living tabernacle in which the Incarnate God was enshrined. She moved about and seemed to outward eyes to be like other holy women. And yet she carried about with her her God as her Child, as the priest carries the Blessed Sacrament. But if the tabernacles in our churches had soul and spirit, if they could understand the Presence within themselves and venerate It, they would become holy in a sense in which they cannot be holy now, and there would be no limit to their growth in sanctity. And yet such was the privilege of Mary, such the rapidity and intensity of her sanctification.

It is easy to see, also, how, from the moment when St. Joseph, at the bidding of the angel, laid aside his hesitation as to his own position with regard to the Blessed Mother and her Child, he also must have had opportunities of advancing in holiness second only to hers. He was living day and night in the sanctuary. He was tending, serving, providing for, and communing with the Incarnate God and His mother. We cannot doubt that his perpetual homage and prayer must have enriched his mind with wonderful illumination as time went on and as Our Lord spoke secretly to the heart of a saint so dear to Himself.

It is not much to suppose that when St. Joseph was allowed to know the Presence of his Lord so close to him and to know also his own most intimate relation and office in the mystery, he too was enabled by God to enter into the heavenly marvel, to understand what it was that had taken place, Who was the Child in the womb of Mary, to adore His divinity, to venerate the gifts of His humanity, and to see in them the ever-flowing and inexhaustible source of blessings and graces for the whole human race.

The contemplation of the divine mysteries connected with the Incarnation must have been an occupation which absorbed all the thoughts and affections of Our Lady and her blessed spouse during the interval between the Visitation and the Nativity. They might have said, like the Apostles on the mountain of the Transfiguration, that it was good for them to be there. The days passed rapidly on, and there was no lack of food for the soul in the considerations which the mystery suggested.

Our Lady and her blessed spouse were deeply read in the Sacred Scriptures, and it is most natural to think that they had received unusual illumination from the understanding of the prophecies. The place of the birth of the promised Child had been as clearly foretold as His birth of a virgin, or His descent from David and Juda. When the Wise Kings came to Jerusalem to ask for the King of the Jews, there was no doubt on the part of the official representatives of the Jewish Church as to the answer which they ought to give to the question of Herod, Where the Christ was to be born? If it was so well known to the learned men at Jerusalem that Bethlehem was the appointed spot, it is not likely that Mary and Joseph were ignorant of the same truth. And yet the months rolled on, and they were still at Nazareth. Our Lady must have known the very time at which the Divine Birth would take place, and St. Joseph must have had the knowledge from her, if not before, at least after the revelation made to him by the angel as to the part which he was to take in the administration of the divine mystery of the Incarnation. Yet the autumn waned and the winter was nigh at hand, and no sign came to them as to any change of residence.

Here again we see the characteristic abandonment of themselves to the providence of God, which has already met us in the lives of these glorious saints. Mary had left herself in His hands as to the great question of her marriage and her virginal vow, and again, she had abandoned herself entirely to the same providence in her silence as to the mystery of the Incarnation when it came about. St. Joseph had been guided at once by the word of the angel, though only conveyed to him in a dream, in the great matter of his perplexity after the Incarnation. And now, how was the Child, over which he had been appointed to watch, to be born at Bethlehem? Was it to be his duty to anticipate any heavenly direction and take on himself to secure, by an act of his own, the fulfillment of the prophecy? If he asked his blessed spouse, it is not likely that he would have found in her any encouragement to independent action. It was enough for them to leave all these things to God. So their simple preparations for the expected birth were made as if they thought it might take place at Nazareth.

The solution to the difficulty was brought about in God's own way. The hearts of kings and of the rulers of the world are all in His hand, and while they think they are carrying out their own schemes of wise policy, so often fraught with cruelties and hardships to those who are placed under them by God as their subjects, they are in truth only bringing about the wise purpose of their Master and Judge. There was a great fitness in the arrangement of Providence, whereby, just at that time, Augustus had decreed the enrollment and possible taxation of all the subjects of the Roman Empire, and whereby also, as far as human causes are concerned, it came about that Our Lord was born in the city of David at Bethlehem. He Who was to be born was the true King of all the world, for nowhere could He be without being King, and moreover, His inheritance of the throne of David could not be more signally attested than by His birth in the holy city. He was, even as Man, an independent Sovereign by right and could owe no allegiance like other men to the sovereign of the world at Rome. And yet it was to be a maxim of His religion, and the constant rule of His Church, that subjects were to obey their rulers, for the sake of conscience, as having authority from God, the Author of human society.

"And it came to pass in those days there went out a decree from Cæsar Augustus that the whole world should be enrolled. This enrolling was first made by Cyrinus the governor of Syria. And all went to be enrolled, every one into his own city."

St. Joseph and his blessed spouse read the will of God, and the solution of their difficulties in the decree of the distant emperor. There was some hardship in a decree which obliged them to a long journey, to a place where they may have had relations, but to which they were practically strangers. But the hand of God was in this decree, and they obeyed it with the utmost joy. It was, indeed, a confirmation to them of the unsleeping care of God over His servants, and for the fulfillment of His own counsels and prophecies.

We are quite ignorant of the distance of time between the announcement of the edict of the emperor and the first Christmas Day. It would take some time for the tidings to reach every little town in a remote province. But Bethlehem and its neighborhood were haunted with the memories and legends connected with the childhood of the great King whose Son was to reign on his throne forever. But above all, the birth at Bethlehem was to them the beginning of a fresh stage in the unfolding of the counsel of God in the dispensation of the Incarnation.

It must be remembered, also, that not even the tranquil and intense joys of the nine months which were now drawing to their close could satisfy the tender and overwhelming longing with which Mary and Joseph must have desired the moment of the Divine Birth. All mothers naturally long for that moment of joy. These natural longings for the birth of their children in the daughters of Eve are the faintest reflections of the yearnings of Mary to see the birth of Our Lord. It was not a man but the Savior of men that was to be born; it was her Child Who had been for so many months her joy and delight, with Whom she had for so long held the sweetest interior conversation and communion. The whole history of the world, since the fall of man, had been a history of longing, on the part of the saints of God, for the moment of the Birth which was now about to take place, and the Fathers speak as if the desires and prayers of those saints had helped on the arrival of that blessed time. But no one of the Patriarchs or Prophets could have prayed so fervently or longed so earnestly for the first Christmas as Our Lady herself. Her long communing with the Sacred Heart had made her own heart its copy and reflection, and she could enter into the desire of Our Lord to begin the work of the Redemption and the instruction of the world, as no one else could understand it.

And with St. Joseph also it was the same as with Mary. He, too, most ardently desired to see the Holy Child over Whom he was to watch, more ardently even than the aged Simeon, who was so soon to hold Him in his arms in the Temple. To Mary and Joseph the time of the Nativity was to be a fresh beginning of their work, for then was to begin

His manifestation to the world, in which manifestation they were to be as His ministers and official servants. The great work had, indeed, already begun, but it was as yet known only to few, and so could affect, consciously, only few. It would be as the sunrise of the new creation, the breaking of the clouds which enwrapped His Infancy by the light of the Sun of Justice. It was a moment awaited with eagerness by the angels, who were ready to hang over the lowly crib and fill heaven and earth with their songs of joy. All over the world there was a hush of peace, as on the eve of some wonderful renovation.

At whatever interval, before the actual moment for leaving Nazareth, Mary and Joseph became aware of the decree of the emperor, their preparations for the necessary journey would not take long to make. And so Mary and Joseph set out alone with their God, full of joy and desire.

Our meditations on the journey to Bethlehem usually dwell on the hardships and sufferings of the day, on the possibilities of inhospitable reception on the road, as well as at Bethlehem, on the anxieties of St. Joseph, on the gentleness, patience, and charity of our Blessed Lady. These things are all true, but they represent only one side of that beautiful picture. Even to ordinary human hearts, which are full of the prospect of some very great joy in sight, the anticipations of the coming happiness are wont to overwhelm all feelings of difficulty, to make all obstacles seem as nothing, and turn all suffering into joy. The holy pair may not have perfectly divined beforehand all the circumstances of humiliation and mortification which, in the providence of God, were to surround the Infant Savior on His first entrance into the world. But they were already full of heavenly light as to the immense condescension of God in becoming a Child in a virgin's womb, and to those accustomed to the contemplation of such condescension, it would not seem much more if He were indeed to choose the utmost poverty and privation for His companions from the very first.

There are legends concerning the prodigies which occurred in various parts of the world—a fountain of oil flowing at Rome, flowers and vines budding and bearing fruit at Ergaddi, and others of the like kind. Although the stories do not appear to rest on any certain evidence, and may be accounted for in other ways, we may take them as signifying the universal expectation of the world, and even of inanimate nature, before the coming of Our Lord. It is natural to think that there may have been some manifestations of this kind, but whether this was so or not, there is no doubt that the event which was about to take place was the dawn of an unexampled renovation and elevation of the whole world. It is certain that the whole race of mankind yearned for its Savior. For Our Lord had already been on earth for many months, and He Who is the light of the world might well kindle with joy at His Presence any who shared in the partial possession of the illumination that came from Him.

And if St. Paul could speak of the whole physical universe as conscious and alive to its own needs, and their coming satisfaction, it is not much to think that even in that lower universe, there may have been some witness vouchsafed to the advent of the Desire of the whole world. Our Lord had come at the Annunciation, but it had been as the seed which is hidden in the earth. Now the time was at hand for the appearance of the little blade which is the first manifestation of the life and fruitfulness of the seed and which causes more joy in the heart of the anxious husbandman than even the ear and the full corn which afterward follow.

This was the peculiar joy of the first Christmas, and we must add this characteristic to the desire of our Blessed Lady on the journey of which we are now speaking. Her presence at Bethlehem had now been brought about in a marvelous and providential manner, and thus the last hindrance to the perfect fulfillment of the prophecies was removed, just as the day approached for the natural termination of the first stage of Our Lord's human existence in her sacred womb. This divine arrangement must have filled her heart with joy and quickened the clearness of her hope. Her desires might now be let loose, might fall on the long-expected moment when she should be able to clasp Our Lord to her heart and gaze upon His face and claim as her own all the sweet joys of complete motherhood. The inconveniences of the journey were little indeed in comparison. The time had come, and she was fast approaching the appointed spot. Could she have foreseen, as she entered Bethlehem, the reception she was to meet with from the inhabitants of the city of David, she might have sorrowed tenderly for them, but she would have felt very little for herself.

The Heart of Our Lord gathered up in His own affections all her yearnings and desires, the yearnings and desires of the whole human world, and of the universe itself. How glorious was to be that renovation which was to have its source in Him. He could see in everything He had made the want of that greater perfection and the craving for that more true and abiding beauty. He had made the human world His own by becoming Man. All was to be renovated and elevated, and the principle of the renovation and elevation which were to come lay in His own humanity.

Over that human world the eyes of the future Savior fell with unutterable love. It was a wild and a tangled maze of degradation and misery, of ignorance where there should have been knowledge of God, of darkness where there should have been light. To the Heart of the Savior of mankind there was nothing, even in all that wilderness of abominations, which did not move the most intense and tender pity. He saw, in all the aberrations of men, the mischief which they generated rather than the guilt which they involved. He read in their most lowering passions, in their most wanton and barbarous excesses, only their need of the redemption which He came to bring them. The louder the cry of sin and pride and hate rose before the throne of heaven, the more deeply did it pierce His Heart as an appeal for help and light and healing and mercy. The maddest ravings of blasphemy sounded to Him as the most piteous appeals for mercy and relief. On the cross, He was to say of His murderers, "Father forgive them, for they know not what they do!" and now the whole world of sin and crime was crying out to heaven for the enlightenment of its ignorances and the pardoning of its sins. He fastened, now as then, on every element in the misery of man which could be pleaded as man's excuse.

In the depths of moral degradation, He read only the need of redemption. His eyes sounded all those depths, and they did not quail before the frightful glare of the hell to which they led. He would fain have quenched it for them entirely in His own Blood. All over the world He saw the evil in a clearness of deformity and a nakedness of malice which would have appalled any but the Savior. He saw the evil only to compassionate it; He rejoiced in the faintest good that He might foster it and strengthen it. He came now not to judge but to save, and He took into His Heart with infinite tenderness every single feature in the moral condition of mankind which called for healing.

He understood all that had been from the beginning of the world of heavenly conversation and of holy aspiration. All these He took up into His own perfect supplication before the throne of His Father, along with the prayers of Mary and Joseph and the living saints of the holy people, who were then more than ever prompted by the Holy Ghost to pour out their hearts in "groanings" ever more intense as they recognized that the appointed time was at hand. But it was not only that the prayers of the saints who were then to be found among the chosen people were then collected in the Sacred Heart and enforced by the strength and might of His own intercession. He was the Lord and Head, not of one generation or nation only, but of all mankind, those who had passed already through the gates of death, and those who were hereafter to enter by the portal of life. Millions of souls were awaiting in the world beyond the grave the consummation of their redemption by His sacrifice, and the supplications and yearnings of the ancient saints, still praying in Limbus, the vast crowds with whom purgatory was filled, and the infants without number who had passed away with the sign of the covenant upon them, all were included in the great ocean of supplication which broke continually before the throne of the Majesty on High. All these prayers and desires were present to the Heart of the Redeemer, as well as the needs of the numberless generations who were to pass through the scene of man's probation after the Redemption had been fully wrought.

Now also when the time had arrived when this new great step was to be taken of the Birth into the world at Bethlehem, it may be thought that He would sum up and make perfect what had been His work while in the womb of Mary and offer it to His Father with His the most tender and reverential love.

The obedience and humiliation of the nine months were on the eve of their accomplishment. His Sacred Body was formed perfect from the very beginning, and the glorious existence to which it had a right, had already been laid aside for the time in order that it might be the fitting Body of Him Who was to be like us in all things, sin only excepted, and Who was to suffer on the cross for the salvation of the world. The Life which He had led in the womb was a Life of intense self-abasement. This had enabled Him to make Himself more completely nothing in the presence of His God and Creator, and thus had added a new beauty to the homage which He had paid to Him. It was this worship of God on the part of the sacred humanity which had added a fresh dignity to the whole creation from the first moment of His Incarnation. God had at last been honored by a worship worthy of Himself and rendered to Him by a created human nature. A human mind had received all that could be known of God. All His revelation of Himself in the universe, and a human heart had given back to the Creator the homage of a perfect love and a gratitude equal to His gifts, honoring Him as He deserved to be honored, praising Him as He deserved to be praised, and making to Him the joyful sacrifice of the perfect surrender and oblation of Itself to His glory. This had now begun in the Sacred Heart, and it was never to cease. It was to spread from Him all over the human race, heart after heart was to catch the flame, which was to fill the whole universe forever.

The Sacred Heart had now been filled with another great and overwhelming passion. The eternal counsel of God for the redemption of the world by His own sufferings had been presented to Him at the first and accepted most willingly and obediently. The offence to God, the mischief to man, the triumph to hell involved in sin, not only in general, but in each particular transgression of all that ever were to be, had been fully counted up. All the arrangements of the Church were rehearsed in the Sacred Heart in its retirement with God. Our Lord was to come forth, when He did come forth, with His work and its instruments all prepared in His Heart beforehand, all steeped in the prayers of the nine months.

Nor had He left Himself without a work of most intense actual perfection in the souls most near to Him. The Baptist leaping in the womb of St. Elizabeth witnesses to the truth and efficacy of this activity of Our Lord. This opens to us a whole world of the operations of grace which followed on His Presence in the womb of Mary. She herself was of course the greatest recipient of His grace, the most intelligent and faithful in her correspondence to the mighty blessings which that Presence brought home to her in an ever increasing stream, and her sanctification during this time was a work of

His which had no parallel in all that He had done in heaven or on earth. He had perfectly fitted her for her great office, as far as its duties had yet come into play, and prepared her for all that was yet to be. In the same way, He had brought about the sanctifications next to hers in their magnificence and beauty of St. Joseph and St. John, and all around, on those who had had any contact with Him in any way, any communication with His mother, any intelligence of or share in the mystery, He had shed profusely and lovingly the gifts of grace which fitted them for the work they might have to do. Who, indeed, can tell how large His bounty may have been in the preparation and sanctification of souls during this sacred time?

And now all was prepared. The Sacred Heart was burning with His own intense but tranquil fire of love for God and man, and for the next onward step in the advance of His work. The appointed days were drawing to their close. He had breathed into the heart of His mother a longing, even more forcible than before, for the moment of the Nativity, and her prayers had long been rising up to heaven for the accomplishment of the mystery. The world was at peace. The hearts most dear to God were full of unwonted cravings, inspired by the Holy Ghost, the great master of prayer. In the far East, the pious kings, if the star had not appeared to them at the date of the Incarnation itself, were watching the heavens for some sign of what they had so much reason to expect. Bethlehem, indeed, was not ready. Its people had no thought of who the strangers were who were drawing near its gates. But the place of which "the Lord had need" was ready, for no one would have thought of disputing with St. Joseph for the tenancy of the cave and the stable. Our Lord lay tranquil and obedient in the womb of Mary, waiting only for the moment appointed by the will of His Father, to step forth into the world of which He was the King, leaving to her, as a parting gift of His power, the unsullied and untouched virginity which His Presence had consecrated forever.